MW00635955

"When it comes to effective crisis management, there is no substitute for experience in the trenches. Jeff Hunt has been tested in some of the toughest crisis situations, from his earliest days in Seoul, Korea to later experiences in Mexico, Latin America, and Europe. *Brand Under Fire* is a must-read for any C-suite officer, particularly with the new realities of the digital age significantly amplifying the threat."

—**Thomas D. Bell Jr.,** Chairman, Mesa Capital Partners

"Corporate directors provide a service by challenging assumptions and the preparedness of their organizations—far in advance of a crisis. Jeff Hunt offers invaluable strategic advice for board members and other leaders of entities that bear enormous responsibility for public safety."

—**Lady Barbara Thomas Judge,** Deputy Chair of the TEPCO Nuclear Reform Monitoring Committee, former Chair of the UK Institute of Directors and the UK Atomic Energy Authority, former member of the US Securities and Exchange Commission, and Non-Executive Director of the LIXIL Group Corporation

BRAND UNDER FIRE

3 THINGS YOU

1: THE SIX STAGES OF A CRISIS

1 Surprise
Your next decision could make or break your career.

2 Insufficient Information
You can't know everything, but share what you do.

3 Intense Scrutiny from the Outside
If you don't fill the information vacuum, someone else will do it for you.

4 Escalating Flow of Events
Things will probably get worse before they get better.

5 Siege Mentality
Craft the narrative you want to project, and demonstrate it through action.

6 The Urge to Bunker Down
Don't do it!

EED TO KNOW

2: THE FIVE KEY PRINCIPLES OF EFFECTIVE CRISIS MANAGEMENT

Authenticity
Be genuine and demonstrate a human touch in every brand interaction.

Transparency
The primary question is not if, but how and when to disclose information.

Speed
Communicate early and often to fill the vacuum and correct misinformation.

Agility
Be prepared to adapt tactics and messaging as the crisis unfolds.

Creativity
Leverage self-published content to tell your story across multiple platforms.

3: THE INFORMATION VACUUM

In a crisis, everyone wants information. An information vacuum will form almost immediately. If you don't fill it, someone else will. You can become *the* source of news by communicating early and often.

BRAND UNDER FIRE

A NEW PLAYBOOK *for* CRISIS MANAGEMENT *in the* DIGITAL AGE

JEFF ROBERT HUNT

with GEOFFREY LEAVENWORTH

ORDNANCE HILL PUBLISHING™

Published by Ordnance Hill Publishing™
Copyright ©2018 Jeff Robert Hunt and Geoffrey Leavenworth
www.BrandUnderFire.com
All rights reserved.

ICF, Inc.
Attn: Office of the General Counsel
9300 Lee Highway
Fairfax, VA 22031

Cover design by Sheila Parr
Book design and composition by Sheila Parr
Illustrations by Joan Hardt

Cataloging-in-Publication data is available.
Print ISBN: 978-0-9995484-0-0
Ebook ISBN: 978-0-9995484-1-7

Printed in the United States of America
17 18 19 20 21 22 23   10 9 8 7 6 5 4 3 2 1
Second Edition

CONTENTS

Described by *PR Week* as "the century's most influential PR figure,"
Harold Burson has served as advisor and confidant to numerous CEOs,
political leaders, and not-for-profit executives. He is the cofounder of
Burson-Marsteller, the world's largest public relations agency. He has
received numerous awards and honors for his contributions to the public
relations industry, as well as to the arts, education, and the humanities.
Photo by Paul Schneck

NAVIGATING THE SHOALS
OF UNCERTAINTY

It can be truly said that the level of uncertainty and its ability to expand into complex crisis situations have never been more widespread for business the world over. Nor has the threat been more universally known to and feared by the populace on every continent. Even a scant review of news coverage of business would indicate that the spread and depth of knowledge by a large segment of the population has generated a fear for the continuance of the way of life that is at the heart of democratic institutions.

One factor that contributes to the severity of this debilitating phenomenon is that many, if not most, businesses and other institutions in our society (including government) have not prepared themselves to cope with major crisis situations. And since negative news attracts more attention than reports of positive developments, the public (and government officials) often overreact to the incident, thereby creating a threat to the reasonable application of law and order deportment.

Notwithstanding numerous books and other data on the issues involved, Jeff Hunt's new account of recent crisis situations, *Brand Under Fire*, serves not only as a reminder that the public is alert to negative news inspired by adverse business conduct, either planned or accidental, but, even more so on how it will affect them in their relationship with the perpetrator as an employee, neighbor, or customer dependent on their product or service. The reader will discern that the "bad guys" are not always the private sector corporations; in many instances the negative result is a factor of unintended consequences resulting from well-intended legislation or regulation.

Jeff Hunt is well-qualified to report on this issue. His career in public relations began with what became an 18-year stint at Burson-Marsteller (for a time his office was next door to mine). He climbed the firm's executive ladder, serving a broad range of clients including DuPont, IBM, Coca-Cola, AT&T, Johnson & Johnson, McDonald's, and Motorola. He was general manager of our offices in Seoul and Mexico City, European chief operating officer based in London, and head of our Latin American region based in Miami. He left us because he wanted to return to Texas, where he took over the well-established Read-Poland firm and went on to become partner and cofounder of PulsePoint Group.

You will find *Brand Under Fire* easy reading, and as a result of this book, you'll know more about how corporations should respond to crises in a manner that serves their best interests with their various constituencies, including employees, customers, shareowners, regulators and legislators, the media, and the general public.

Harold Burson
February 17, 2017

Larry Scott is the Commissioner of the Pac-12 Conference. He is the former CEO of the Women's Tennis Association (WTA) and former chief operating officer of the Association of Tennis Professionals (ATP), which operates the men's professional tennis tour. He was captain of the Harvard tennis team and played professionally on the ATP circuit.

INTRODUCTION

I welcome the publication of *Brand Under Fire* because I know first-hand how valuable Jeff Hunt's insights have been to me and to the CEOs and leaders of many other organizations facing crises.

Jeff and I met in London nearly 20 years ago. I was chief operating officer for the Association of Tennis Professionals (ATP), and he was COO for Burson-Marsteller in Europe. Throughout our long relationship, I have come to depend on Jeff's judgment, strategic insight, and creativity to help resolve conflicts and crises in the high-profile world of sports management.

Jeff and his superb team at ICF practice intelligent, evidence-based communication strategy, with a deep understanding of digital platforms and the analytics to measure performance. Jeff's expertise has helped me and scores of other business leaders to navigate the new communications landscape dominated by digital and social media. It's an environment where an issue or a full-blown crisis can explode in minutes rather than hours. He and his team have mastered digital technology and analysis of the online conversation and social media. I can depend on his experience and knowledge to help me reach critical decisions at any hour and anywhere on the planet.

Furthermore, while he has helped me in highly visible situations, some of his best work occurred behind the scenes to resolve issues *before* they made headlines. His analysis of the six stages of a crisis should be required reading for anyone dealing with a serious public relations challenge.

In my world, athletes often quickly transition from private citizens to highly scrutinized public figures. Few people come fully equipped to adapt to the glare of celebrity. Jeff has helped quarterback Cam Newton, tennis champion Maria Sharapova, and golfers Dustin Johnson and Jordan Spieth prepare for the limelight. He has also helped more experienced athletes, such as Venus and Serena Williams, craft and convey key messages effectively.

In my roles as chief executive of major sports organizations, Jeff has helped me deal with such challenging issues as gambling, doping, gender equality, and discrimination.

When I was CEO of the Women's Tennis Association (WTA) in 2006, I made equal prize money for women at Wimbledon a cornerstone of my leadership agenda. Jeff mapped out a strategy to communicate our message, reach out to key constituents, and give the players a strong voice in the public debate. Jeff helped us stay positive in our negotiations, win public support, protect our brand, and ultimately prevail. Within a year, the women were playing for equal prize money.

A few years later, we developed the first WTA tournament in Dubai with the understanding that all qualifying players could participate, regardless of nationality or religion. A few days before the tournament, we received word that the Israeli player Shahar Peer would not be receiving a promised visa to enter the country. We needed to shape a response and a strategy, and we didn't have much time. Moreover, the world was watching, and we were making these decisions under intense pressure.

We decided to conduct the tournament under protest and ultimately fined the tournament promoters $300,000, which was given to charity. Jeff and his team were instrumental in shaping strategy, messaging, and media relations during the incident. The next year the Dubai tournament was open to all nationalities, and Shahar Peer earned a spot in the semifinals. It was an inspiring example of the power of sport to influence society and public policy.

Throughout our long history, Jeff has helped me explore complex issues, identify our most important principles, and take the actions that uphold them. He has also been invaluable in sorting through the complexities of stakeholder relations and internal communications. Jeff has demonstrated to us, and to scores of clients, that in crisis, your core values must be your North Star.

Read *Brand Under Fire* to gain a deeper understanding of the six stages of a crisis and to help you respond with innovative communication strategies for the digital era.

Larry Scott
Pac-12 Conference Commissioner
April 2017

WHY YOU NEED THIS BOOK

Our research shows that while executives recognize the growing importance
of digital and social media influence, corporate America is falling behind in
harnessing these new tools for crisis communications.

52% Only 52% of C-Suite executives say their organization has basic crisis communication strategies in place.

72% 72% of executives agree that managing crisis communication should fundamentally incorporate new strategies and capabilities, but only 20% say their crisis planning has changed "a great deal."

23% Less than a quarter of executives indicate that crisis recovery times for corporate reputations, finances, and operations will be shorter with the growth of digital and social media.

13% Only 13% are "very satisfied" with their ability to monitor online conversations during a crisis.

In future crises, executives indicate the following will likely increase, based on the effects of digital and social media: Costs (64%), connection with insurance premiums (57%), Board of Director involvement (55%), and budgets (53%), but fewer will be hiring staff for crisis preparedness (45%).

Source: Crisis Communications Preparedness in a Digital/Social World, a survey of corporate executives, ICF, December 2016.

PREFACE

Some crises can be prevented, but many cannot. The measure of a chief executive and leader is his or her ability to respond to crisis, regain trust, learn from the experience, and leave the organization stronger for it. This book shares the principles, techniques, and insights to help you make better decisions in crisis and communicate with those whose lives are touched by crisis. It draws on the experience of people who have wrestled with some of the most challenging emergencies ever faced by companies and institutions. And the stakes have never been higher.

After 30 years helping companies around the world manage crisis communications, I have seen a profound shift in strategy with the advent of digital and social media. There has been a great deal of focus on the impact of the digital revolution on marketing and communications but much less about crisis communications. Here's a new playbook for the digital era.

Crises can erupt from many sources: natural disasters, data breaches, workplace violence, financial fraud, product flaws, employee misconduct, industrial accidents—not to mention new threats we haven't discovered.

Mismanage one crisis and your career may be over, your company may be bankrupt, and your work force may be applying for unemployment benefits. Crises have cost people their livelihoods—and their lives.

You may feel that you already have a crisis officer or risk manager on your staff and that combined with your legal counsel, you have the expertise that you need. But risk officers and lawyers tend to focus on operational and legal risk. Their advice can be completely contrary to what's necessary to effectively manage your reputational risk. It's possible to win the legal battle and severely damage your reputation in the process.

The purpose of this book is to arm you with the principles, tools, and strategies to navigate the most challenging situations. It explores the essential characteristics of effective crisis management: authenticity, transparency, speed, agility, and creativity.

You will learn to identify the six stages of crisis. Each stage is a potential trap to lure you into paralysis and inaction. These are the normal reactions and conditions that people and organizations experience when facing an emergency:

1. Surprise
2. Insufficient Information
3. Intense Scrutiny from the Outside
4. Escalating Flow of Events
5. Siege Mentality
6. The Urge to Bunker Down

THE SIX STAGES OF A CRISIS

 **Surprise**
Your next decision could make
or break your career.

 Insufficient Information
You can't know everything,
but share what you do.

 **Intense Scrutiny from
the Outside**
If you don't fill the information
vacuum, someone else will do it
for you.

 Escalating Flow of Events
Things will probably get worse
before they get better.

 **Siege Mentality**
Craft the narrative you want
to project, and demonstrate it
through action.

 The Urge to Bunker Down
Don't do it!

Having the presence of mind to know where you are in this unfamiliar landscape will help you overcome fear, anxiety, and inertia—and move forward.

Why should you listen to me? I've had the opportunity to advise CEOs and communications executives in some of the greatest crises of the last four decades. These include the Penn State public relations disaster unleashed by the sexual abuse of children by former football coach Jerry Sandusky; the Fukushima catastrophe involving the meltdown of Japanese nuclear reactors in the wake of a massive earthquake and tsunami; and one of the nation's largest banking scandals.

I have also advised some of the nation's largest companies on crisis preparedness. My team at ICF and I have helped them establish advance warning systems to manage issues and crises, using sophisticated listening tools to keep them ahead of threats to their businesses and reputations. We have conducted realistic crisis simulations that train CEOs and corporate leadership to apply these principles and implement these strategies *in advance* of crisis.

And while most of my work has involved business organizations, I've also helped athletes, many of them young people facing public scrutiny for the first time. I have coached professional tennis players Serena and Venus Williams and Maria Sharapova, golfers Dustin Johnson and Jordan Spieth, and NFL quarterback Cam Newton on developing their public personas, shaping key messages, interacting with the media, and building their reputations.

In addition, I've turned to experts from various sectors that must respond to crisis, including legal affairs, government relations, international business, higher education, and the White House. Their insights appear as sidebars within these chapters.

In the majority of the cases shared in these pages, I have first-hand knowledge from my work with the clients involved or because the situations I describe were handled by my mentors or colleagues. While I am loath to second-guess good people struggling with challenging situations, I'll share the inside stories and the resulting insights that will help arm you for battle.

You will learn how the digital revolution has created opportunities to create your own content that can compete with conventional and new media, giving you the chance to tell your story directly to your stakeholders. I'll also show you how to develop your own outlets for sharing accurate information to fill the information vacuum and position your brand as the leading source for dependable information throughout the crisis.

Effective communication strategies require more than just crafting strategic messages and sharing those messages with your most important constituencies. They include telling the story of how you are going to respond to crisis, taking action to prevent it from happening again, and correcting the product or process in such a way that people benefit from what you've learned.

In every good story there is a villain, a victim, a hero, and a moral. You need to cast your story in such a way that your actions make it clear that you are part of the solution—even if you started the narrative as the villain. Your story emphasizes that you are making a heroic effort to make things right.

Responding to crisis is not about spin, it's about taking action that exemplifies your values. The following chapters will show you how.

Jeff Robert Hunt

1

COMPANIES IN PERIL

"By the time you hear the thunder, it's too late to build the ark."
—*Unknown*

Martin Winterkorn was having a stressful evening. But he had no idea it would be his last as chief executive of global giant Volkswagen. After all, he was the highest paid executive in Germany and one of the most powerful and influential corporate heads in Europe. Under Winterkorn's leadership, Volkswagen had set its sights on becoming the largest carmaker in the world. And with a bold gamble in China, he might just succeed.

At 68, Winterkorn was said to be a severe taskmaster with a distant management style who leveraged "fear and respect" to get things done. Earlier that day, he had apologized on behalf of Volkswagen in response to a report that the company had designed software to generate deceptive emissions reports in its diesel cars. The event may have left him with a case of indigestion, but overall, Winterkorn was still in command. He was defiant in responding to calls for a shake-up at VW, blaming the emissions scandal on "the mistakes of a few people" and stating, "I am not aware of any wrongdoing on my part."

But a day after vowing to manage the crisis, Winterkorn was history. The VW board forced him out on September 23, 2015, and the downward spiral of Volkswagen continued. The company's market capitalization plunged by about one-third—or 25 billion euros—in the 48 hours after it admitted that 11 million of its cars had been designed to cheat during emissions testing. A bloodbath of additional executive firings ensued.

In an astonishing admission in *The New York Times*, VW's communications chief Hans-Gerd Bode said in an interview five months after the crisis hit: "There was something like a tsunami, thousands of calls and emails coming in at the same time. A crisis like this, the company was not prepared for. . . . We don't know the right way out."

When the Harris Poll conducted its annual survey of Americans' perceptions of corporate reputations in early 2016, Volkswagen came in dead last, ranking 100th out of 100 companies included in the survey. As for its goal of achieving world domination, Volkswagen watched its sales plunge with the next quarter's results. The scandal also threatened the company's Porsche, Audi, and other global brands.

"THERE WAS SOMETHING LIKE A **TSUNAMI**, THOUSANDS OF CALLS AND EMAILS COMING IN AT THE SAME TIME. A CRISIS LIKE THIS, THE COMPANY WAS NOT PREPARED FOR. . . . WE DON'T KNOW THE RIGHT WAY OUT."

Volkswagen's decision to adopt a contrite posture in the US but a defiant one in Europe ignored the ease with which information is now shared globally and proved disastrous. In the US, where Volkswagen acknowledged that it had broken the law, it quickly began making amends through "goodwill packages" containing gift cards, free service at VW dealers, and a free roadside service program. But in Europe, where the company claims its deception did not violate the law, car owners received nothing. European customers and lawmakers were outraged.

Meanwhile, $7 billion was set aside to cover the cost of recalls, fines, and litigation in the United States. The executive team's plea that it didn't know what was happening did not ring true and, in any event, was a weak line of defense. It didn't take long for internal emails to emerge that implied that the corporate leadership knew of problems with its auto emissions a year before the public disclosures. All of these revelations were shared across the globe with blinding speed because of the power of social media.

This cascade of bad judgment delivered the headline from hell in England's *Daily Telegraph*: "Volkswagen Emissions Scandal Could Kill 200 Britons." Volkswagen couldn't have bought such catastrophic publicity if it had tried.

In every crisis, the way companies and their executives respond—and communicate their actions—is critical to the outcome. How corporations respond to all their stakeholders in the aftermath of calamity can be of greater long-term impact than the actual event that triggered the crisis. Reputational injury to a brand, or a company, can be fatal.

In every crisis, the way companies and their executives respond—and communicate their actions—is critical to the outcome. How corporations respond to all their stakeholders in the aftermath of calamity can be of greater long-term impact than the actual event that triggered the crisis. Reputational injury to a brand, or a company, can be fatal.

When BP's Deepwater Horizon offshore rig exploded in 2010, it triggered what has been described as the nation's worst environmental disaster. The explosion itself killed 11 people and destroyed the rig. More than three million barrels of crude oil fouled beaches and wetlands from Florida to Texas, although CEO Tony Hayward described the spill almost a month later as "relatively tiny." BP's early response—minimizing the size of the spill and discounting the environmental impact—exacerbated the situation and contributed to the $18.7 billion in state and federal fines it was forced to pay, on top of the $44 billion spent on legal and cleanup costs. CEO Hayward, harshly criticized for his tone-deaf statements early in the crisis, and for conspicuously going sailing and complaining "I want my life back," was fired. "I can't possibly know why the decisions were made . . . because I wasn't there," he explained in Congressional testimony two months after the explosion. BP experienced a terrible accident, but much of the damage to its reputation in the early weeks of the crisis was self-inflicted.

THE CATASTROPHIC COST OF SILENCE

The Enron securities fraud crisis led to the convictions and imprisonment of its president and other top executives. Twenty-three thousand Enron employees lost their jobs and much of the value of their pensions. And $63 billion in shareholder value evaporated in what was then the largest corporate bankruptcy in America. Enron's 64-year-old CEO Ken Lay died while awaiting sentencing for 10 criminal convictions for fraud, conspiracy, and making false statements. Meanwhile the fiasco took down the venerable 89-year-old accounting firm of Arthur Andersen and the jobs of its 85,000 employees. The devastation extended to Enron's banks, business partners, and investors, as well public pension and endowment funds with large stakes in the company.

It's tempting to conclude that Enron was less a communications crisis than the natural consequence of criminal behavior. But had the leadership accepted responsibility for the mistakes—and then taken action to address them—the outcome could have been much less disastrous. Everyone—even the wrongdoers—would have benefited from more honesty and transparency in the aftermath of the crisis.

The 2013 security breach at retailer Target resulted in more than $250 million in fines, an estimated $500 million in other costs, and the departure of its CEO and chief information officer. The company took a "quiet approach" in responding to the hacking incident, initially reporting it to the government but not informing customers. Target was also less than forthcoming in acknowledging that it had ignored the early warning signs of a breach. The episode, which unfolded during the hectic November–December holiday season, resulted in the personal information of some 70 million customers being stolen at a time when shoppers felt especially vulnerable.

Three customers died and at least 10 were sickened from contaminated Blue Bell ice cream in 2015. The people who died were served ice cream as patients in a Kansas hospital. Every Blue Bell product in every store and food service outlet had to be pulled from the shelves, and the company's sales came to a screeching halt.

Had the leadership accepted responsibility for the mistakes—and then taken action to address them— the outcome could have been much less disastrous. Everyone—even the wrongdoers—would have benefited from more honesty and transparency in the aftermath of the crisis.

The tragedy almost destroyed the company. Indeed, one third of Blue Bell employees lost their jobs and another third were furloughed. Interestingly, no executives are known to have been fired, which may be attributable to Blue Bell's status as a privately held company. But the effect on the treasured ice cream maker was profound. A major equity position was sold to an investor group including the Bass Brothers in exchange for a cash infusion necessary to save the 108-year-old family business. Blue Bell Creameries is now under criminal investigation by the US Department of Justice regarding the handling of the contamination incident by its management.

Beloved brands such as Blue Bell are just as susceptible to a public relations crisis. In fact, they are held to a higher standard and subjected to greater scrutiny *because* they are beloved by their stakeholders. Strong emotional engagement with your customers raises consumer expectations.

CRISIS IN A RADICALLY CHANGED WORLD

The world has changed. The digital revolution has raised the stakes, making crises even more incendiary and destructive. If you are playing by the old crisis management playbook, you're going to lose.

Social media and other digital platforms have leveled the playing field. Customers, critics, consumer interest groups, and competitors have an arsenal of digital weapons they can use to attack companies under siege.

The traditional 24-hour news cycle has evolved to the nanosecond news cycle, where a story can be published and catch fire in the cyber world moments after an event. Reputations can be savaged in only a few hours when stories go viral. In the court of public opinion, the witnesses, judge, and jury can become anyone with a smartphone. CEOs no longer have the luxury to take a wait-and-see approach once a story has gained traction on social media. Smartphones, social media, and the Internet have made journalists out of everyone. Major stories that have broken on social media include the US raid on the compound of Osama Bin Laden, unknowingly live-tweeted by an observer surprised to see a helicopter hovering overhead, the Boston Marathon bombing, the deadly 2008 Sichuan earthquake in China, and the US Airways airliner that landed in New York's Hudson River.

BELOVED BRANDS ARE JUST AS SUSCEPTIBLE TO A PUBLIC RELATIONS CRISIS. IN FACT, THEY ARE HELD TO A HIGHER STANDARD.

CRISIS IN A RADICALLY CHANGED WORLD

Nanosecond
News Cycle

Local Stories Can
Become Global Stories

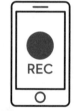

Citizen Journalists

Speed Favored
over Accuracy

Vocal & Disruptive
Minority

"TWITTER IS THE NEW ASSOCIATED PRESS."

—*Dave Samson, General Manager of Public Affairs at Chevron*

"Twitter is the new Associated Press," says Dave Samson, general manager of public affairs at Chevron and chair of the Arthur Page Society, the preeminent international association of senior communications executives. "I can't think of an incident we have faced over the last four years where we didn't learn of it over social media at the same time we were learning of it through our own internal channels. In some cases, we were seeing it in social media channels first."

It's important that we realize what created the rise of social media. A fundamental distrust of institutions and an inherent trust in peer-to-peer communications—combined with technologies that increase the scale of intimacy—gave birth to the social media phenomenon.

A few of the new realities:

- Anyone with a smartphone and a social media account can be a citizen-journalist.

- Social media platforms created new channels for citizen-journalists and bloggers to reach large audiences.

- Citizen-journalists and rogue employees feed the media and serve up content to advance their own agendas, often without any regard for journalistic ethics. Anyone can say anything at any time with no accountability.

- Local stories can rapidly become global stories.

- A vocal minority can now become a powerful media engine.

- Digital tools give the public and the media quick access to fact-checking tools, regulatory documents, safety reports, and other data that can help shape a narrative.

THE COURT OF
PUBLIC OPINION

THE EVOLUTION OF ENGAGEMENT

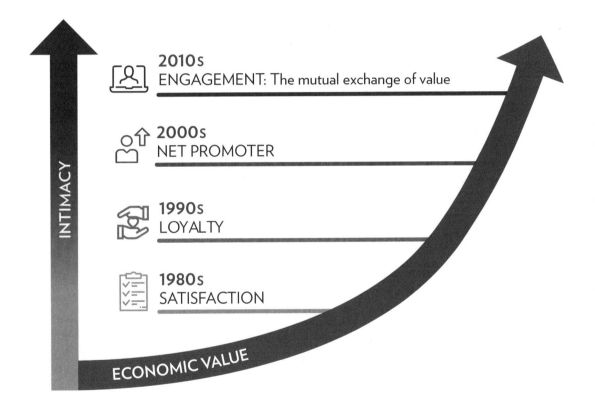

2010s
ENGAGEMENT: The mutual exchange of value

2000s
NET PROMOTER

1990s
LOYALTY

1980s
SATISFACTION

INTIMACY

ECONOMIC VALUE

Intimacy is an organization's ability to interact with consumers in a humanized way. The scale of intimacy has drastically changed since the 1980s. Today, engagement is essential for organizations to ensure a mutual exchange of value with consumers.

- Search engines are powerful research tools for everyone—including adversaries—and they favor fresh and viral content.

- Content providers place a high value on the "shareability" of content, accelerating the spread of information.

While all of these changes present challenges, they also create opportunities for the savvy executive. The decentralized nature of the media and the tools of the digital era make it possible for companies to become their own content factories—disseminating news, background information, video, infographics, and all types of content in real time and on multiple platforms. This provides companies the opportunity to position their messages and tell their story directly to stakeholders without the filter of hostile or poorly informed reporting. While digital tools cannot be a substitute for a media strategy, they enable companies to become producers of timely and reliable content that may be more comprehensive, more accurate, and more user-friendly than conventional media.

But for this strategy to work, your content must be compelling and creative. You can't run away from bad news. For example, during the Dell Computer battery recall, the largest consumer electronics recall at the time, some bloggers and websites were featuring videos of Dell computers bursting into flames from overheated batteries. My team and I, as consultants to Dell, realized this was irresistible content that would attract viewers. So we persuaded Dell to link to the burning laptop video on its own website, giving the company increased credibility and traffic and improved search engine results. As a result, we were able to reach a larger audience with Dell's key messages.

COMPELLING CONTENT WILL GIVE YOU A CHANCE TO TELL YOUR STORY ON YOUR TERMS.

A NEW ECOSYSTEM FOR ENGAGEMENT

Feedback Loop

Digital Listening

Sophisticated social listening technology informs message and content development by capturing relevant digital conversation data. Listening technology also reveals conversations and influencer comments in social media that can be engaged with directly.

Campaign Theme & Objectives

A unifying concept designed to engage key constituents, with actionable and measureable objectives. Created with input from key stakeholders.

Measurement

Robust key performance indicators for every facet of the campaign. Reporting and optimization occurs in real-time, daily, weekly, and monthly.

Conversations

Community managers engage in conversations online with targeted audiences. An opportunity to share content and reinforce positive behaviors.

DIGITAL-FIRST, CONTENT-CENTRIC MODEL FOR ENGAGEMENT

To effectively change perceptions and avoid communicating in an echo chamber, we must build a custom audience engagement plan, aligned to the core components of our tried-and-tested ecosystem for engagement in the age of digital.

Key Messages
Concise, consumable messaging that would inform the development of all content.

Content Creation
Visual, engaging content, designed to capture attention, convey key messages, and be shared easily.

Stories   *Videos*   *Infographics*

Content Dissemination
Owned: Channels owned as part of the campaign. Microsite serves as content hub.

Paid: Traditional & digital platforms supporting paid promotion / advertising.

Earned: Campaign coverage through news operations.

Audience / Channel Optimization
Content is modified for specific audiences (e.g. individuals vs. small business) and modified (e.g. dimensions) for specific channels.

The digital era makes it nearly impossible to hide information for very long. A passionate focus on a company's values, ethics, and character is even more important—in advance of and during a crisis—as a crisis management tool.

It's also important for your communications not to be written in an institutional, legalistic voice when rival channels are being published in the more authentic and personal voice of social media. Compelling content will give you a chance to tell your story on your terms. Hiding behind legalistic jargon deprives you of that opportunity.

MILLENNIALS HAVE INFLUENCED THE REST OF SOCIETY

The Millennial generation has changed the game. In 2015 in the United States there were 92 million Millennials (ages 15–35) compared to 61 million members of Generation X (ages 36–50) and 77 million Baby Boomers (ages 51–70). Millennials have influenced the way we do business not only by their sheer numbers, as the largest generation in American history, but also by their behavior

The digital era makes it nearly impossible to hide information for very long. A passionate focus on a company's values, ethics, and character is even more important—in advance of and during a crisis—as a crisis management tool.

MILLENNIALS

THE FIRST DIGITAL NATIVES

POPULATION IN MILLIONS
PER AGE SEGMENT

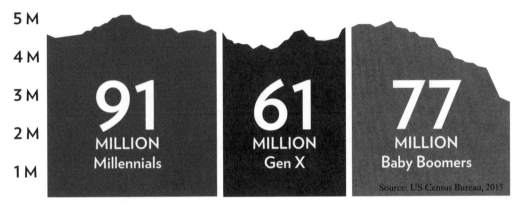

5 M
4 M
3 M
2 M
1 M

91 MILLION Millennials

61 MILLION Gen X

77 MILLION Baby Boomers

Source: US Census Bureau, 2015

15   20   25   30   35 36   40   45   50   51   55   60   65   70

AGE IN 2015

MORE THAN
90%
USE SMARTPHONES

Source: Nielsen Mobile Insights, 2016

SOME
84%
FOLLOW BRANDS
ON FACEBOOK

Source: University of Massachusetts
Dartmouth Center, 2013

ALMOST HALF
WATCH VIDEOS ONLY ON
THEIR MOBILE DEVICE

Source: Omnicom Media Group, 2017

as digital natives. More than 90 percent use smartphones. Some 84 percent of them follow brands on Facebook and almost half watch videos only on their mobile devices. They use the Internet to access product information, consumer reviews, and price comparisons to shop through the most convenient channels and at the most competitive prices.

Millennials consume content differently, and the way they do so has influenced the entire marketplace. They watch entertainment on devices when they want to, not when it's broadcast by the networks or screened by theaters. And they are much more likely to watch "TV" on a desktop, tablet, or smartphone than other generations. Their embrace of mobile devices and digital platforms has rubbed off on the rest of society. That's why you arc almost as likely to see a 65-year-old checking his smartphone at a supermarket or a sporting event as a 25-year-old.

Millennials are more distrustful of conventional news media, and they more frequently turn to peer-influenced media, such as online search engines and social media, for reliable information sources than to newspapers and magazines. That creates an opportunity for companies that use the web and social media to tell their story effectively.

As much as the communications landscape has changed, some things remain steadfast. Authenticity, accuracy, and transparency are still essential. My mentor, Harold Burson, helped create a blueprint for crisis management during the 1982 Tylenol product-tampering saga that we can still learn from today.

In that celebrated case, seven people died after taking cyanide-laced Tylenol. The product's maker, Johnson & Johnson (J&J), quickly removed 31 million bottles of Tylenol from shelves

AUTHENTICITY, ACCURACY, AND TRANSPARENCY ARE STILL ESSENTIAL.

worldwide—$100 million worth of product—and offered a reward for information leading to an arrest. But what was truly extraordinary was the access that CEO James Burke gave to the CBS news program *60 Minutes*. J&J allowed CBS reporters and camera crews into the boardroom during critical strategy sessions, creating an unprecedented level of transparency. The action helped portray J&J as a credible, sympathetic, and responsive entity that was using every means to address the crisis. J&J then developed tamper-resistant packaging that established a new industry standard for product safety. As a result, the price of J&J stock returned to its near-record high within two months of the poisonings, and Tylenol's market share, which took longer to recover, bounced back. James Burke was heralded as an exceptional crisis manager, and the episode has come to be viewed as a textbook example of how to handle a public relations crisis. Burke received the Medal of Freedom from President Bill Clinton and was named one of history's greatest CEOs by *Fortune* magazine. When he died in 2012, his role in the Tylenol case was mentioned favorably in the first sentence of most obituaries, including *The New York Times*.

THE
JOHNSON & JOHNSON
TYLENOL CRISIS

September 29, 1982

Seven people died after taking cyanide-laced Tylenol

Investigators soon determined that the tainted Tylenol capsules hadn't been tampered with at the factories where they were produced

Johnson & Johnson launched a massive public relations campaign urging the public not to use Tylenol

Johnson & Johnson removed 31 million bottles of Tylenol from shelves worldwide and offered a reward for information leading to an arrest

CEO James Burke gave to the CBS news program *60 Minutes* access to the boardroom during critical strategy sessions, creating an unprecedented level of transparency

Johnson & Johnson developed tamper-resistant packaging that established a new industry standard for product safety, and Tylenol was back on store shelves within months

The price of Johnson & Johnson stock returned to its near-record high within two months of the poisonings

Tylenol's market share bounced back

Source: *www.ou.edu/deptcomm/dodjcc/groups/02C2/Johnson%20&%20Johnson.htm*

The stakes could not be higher. If you are adhering to the old rules, you are destined to lose.

The challenge today is to apply the principles exemplified in the Tylenol saga to a world that has changed forever with the advent of digital and social media. The stakes could not be higher. If you are adhering to the old rules, you are destined to lose.

Every crisis is rife with danger and opportunity. You need to be able to recognize the difference, avoiding one and seizing the other through insightful decisions and communications. Your survival, and that of your organization, depends on it.

SURPRISE

Your next decision could make or break your career.

2

THE NANOSECOND NEWS CYCLE

"Don't wait until you're in a crisis to come up with a plan."
—*Phillip Calvin McGraw (Dr. Phil)*

Scott Pendery was experiencing a normal workday at Magnablend, a thriving specialty chemical company in Waxahachie, Texas. Magnablend had recently recapitalized in partnership with private equity firms to finance its expansion. The future looked bright for the company as it produced chemicals for the fracking boom that was dramatically increasing oil and gas production in the United States. But a few minutes before 11:00 a.m. on October 3, 2011, Magnablend's sole manufacturing plant exploded and was engulfed in flames.

Pendery, CEO of the company and the nephew of its founder, suddenly found himself in the vortex of a crisis. He was in stage 1 of crisis—surprise!

A neighboring elementary school, community college, and hundreds of residents near the plant were evacuated—about 1,000 people in all. The Texas National Guard was deployed to help with the crisis.

Minutes after the explosion, dramatic live video showed a fire truck inundated by a flowing river of burning chemicals. Fire fighters had to flee for their lives, sacrificing the $1.2 million fire truck to the conflagration. The plant was leveled, but fortunately—almost miraculously—there were no deaths or injuries.

In the hours that followed, Scott Pendery needed to make many decisions—and confront many questions. The fate of his company and the livelihood of his employees were at stake.

BURNING OUT OF CONTROL

In this case, I was able to arrive in Waxahachie within a few hours of the explosion. One of my associates followed shortly thereafter, and we had several staff in our Austin office working on the situation. As I was traveling to Waxahachie, colleagues in Austin were establishing a digital listening capability to learn what was being reported in conventional media, in social media, on blogs, and elsewhere. We also wanted to know the key topics of conversation and public concern on social media to help inform our messages.

In every crisis, I emphasize five key principles:

Authenticity—Be genuine and demonstrate a human touch in every brand interaction.

Transparency—The primary question now is not if, but how and when to disclose information.

Speed—Communicate early and often to fill the vacuum and correct misinformation.

Agility—Be prepared to adapt tactics and messaging as the crisis unfolds.

Creativity—Leverage self-published content to tell your story across multiple platforms.

Upon arriving at Magnablend, I helped establish a situation room and emphasized the importance of isolating the crisis team from moment-to-moment managerial operations. We all make better decisions when we can focus one key decision at a time instead of trying to juggle everything at once. Isolating the crisis team was difficult in this case because the company's management ranks were lean, and some operational decision-making could not be delegated.

The next task was to create a preliminary statement for external audiences and employees. We needed to share what information we had about the explosion, acknowledge that there was much that we did not know, and emphasize that we would do everything within our power to determine the cause of the accident. We also needed to take responsibility for what had happened, express our concern for people

THE FIVE KEY PRINCIPLES OF EFFECTIVE CRISIS MANAGEMENT

Authenticity
Be genuine and demonstrate a human touch in every brand interaction.

Transparency
The primary question is not if, but how and when to disclose information.

Speed
Communicate early and often to fill the vacuum and correct misinformation.

Agility
Be prepared to adapt tactics and messaging as the crisis unfolds.

Creativity
Leverage self-published content to tell your story across multiple platforms.

affected by the fire, and address our responsibility to the community and to our employees and customers. Finally, we needed to commit to taking necessary actions to make sure that something like this never happened again. My colleague and I gave Scott Pendery and other company executives some quick media training.

We benefited from the fact that Waxahachie was a small town and that Pendery had been a fully engaged member of the community, earning the company a great deal of goodwill within city government, with the school district and community college, and with residents. We were also fortunate that employees were successfully evacuated from the plant without injury and that there were no injuries to firefighters, passersby, or others.

Our digital media listening center in Austin was relaying the key topics of conversation to the situation room to help us develop a communications strategy, which included conducting a press conference. Facing the media was not an instinctive choice on the part of the management and the company's lawyers, who had arrived from Houston. But by doing so, we were able to avoid the perception that Magnablend was withholding information, which could lead to losing the initial sympathetic public sentiment in the Waxahachie community. The press conference placed the emphasis on the company's commitment to supporting the investigation and cooperating with regulatory agencies that were involved. We advised against speculation on the cause of the explosion, which was not then fully understood. There was also enormous concern for the air quality and for the environmental impact of water runoff resulting from the firefighting effort.

The inferno dominated regional news coverage and was reported on the national network news that evening. A YouTube video of the fire truck being destroyed after the firefighters' narrow escape was viewed tens of thousands of times. Television trucks and news helicopters appeared within minutes and, because the decision was made to allow the building to burn itself out, the story stayed alive for days and provided video of the smoldering facilities for the media.

My team and I helped keep the Magnablend management from going into bunker-down mode, a natural inclination toward inaction in the absence of definitive information. You will never have all the information in the heat of crisis. Waiting for more information is a tempting excuse for doing nothing and waiting for the emergency to pass. In this case, it was also important to gain the confidence and support of Magnablend's lawyers. We needed to make our case for holding a press briefing in spite of the fact that we lacked answers to obvious questions such as: What caused the explosion? What chemicals were involved? Who was at fault? How long would it take for the fire to burn itself out?

YOU WILL NEVER HAVE ALL THE INFORMATION IN THE HEAT OF A CRISIS.

The press briefing enabled the company to shape the narrative and help fill the information vacuum.

An important decision was choosing a spokesperson for Magnablend. We considered having the chief chemist speak for the company. But after some debate, we decided that the CEO was the most effective public voice. The company had a reservoir of goodwill within the community, which was closely identified with CEO Scott Pendery. He was related to the founder of the company, and he was well-spoken and knowledgeable. Finally, we were not yet trying to explain the chemical processes involved in the explosion, so we didn't need extensive technical expertise. Scott was the face of the brand in good times, so having him represent the company in crisis made sense. His presence lent authenticity to the briefing and added a familiar human voice.

The press briefing enabled the company to shape the narrative and help fill the information vacuum.

We also were striving to keep the national fracking debate from distorting or magnifying reports of the fire, potentially transforming a local story into a more-enduring national one. Our focus was on what was happening in Waxahachie and how the community and the company would recover. Our efforts helped Magnablend retain its reputation as a good neighbor and responsible corporate citizen in the community. We also used social media to monitor and respond to some of the criticism by environmental groups and potential litigants.

While the media coverage was intense, it was important that

THE INFORMATION VACUUM

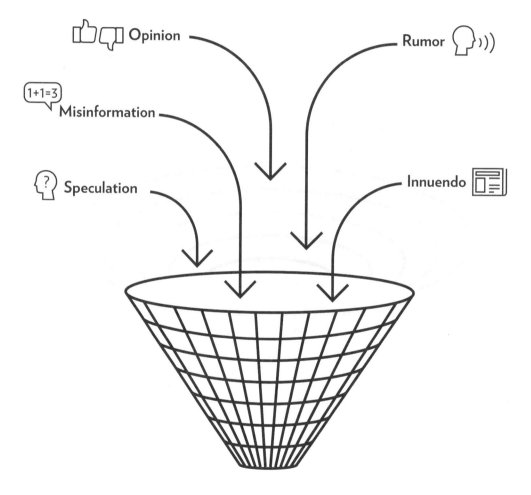

In a crisis, everyone wants information. An information vacuum will form almost immediately. If you don't fill it, someone else will. You can become *the* source of news by communicating early and often.

we communicate effectively with employees. The destruction of the factory created much speculation and anxiety about whether jobs at Magnablend would be lost permanently. During and after the crisis we had to reassure employees that their needs were a high priority and that the company had every intention of rebuilding the factory and resuming operation. Internal communications are often overlooked in a crisis, and it was especially important in a small community where a major employer played such a large role in the local economy.

Magnablend overcame its big surprise in 2011. It rebuilt in a less populated area and was later acquired by the global chemical distribution company, Univar.

The Magnablend explosion occurred before the digital and social media phenomenon had fully developed. But there are several key takeaways from the episode:

- Establish a digital listening command center immediately to provide evidence-based knowledge of the issues in the online conversation and in conventional media.

- Don't be afraid to tell stakeholders what you know—and what you don't know.

- Be assertive in arguing the need for authentic and transparent communications. Sometimes the lawyers will argue against transparency because of liability issues. But it's possible to win a legal battle while losing the reputational war; the latter can be more costly. Effective working relationships between the legal team and the crisis team *before* a crisis can sensitize the lawyers to the need for communication. It also can help establish a rapid approval process for content during a crisis. This is especially important in heavily regulated industries such as banking or pharmaceuticals, where in addition to civil liability there are complex regulatory restrictions regarding communications, as well as in publicly traded companies subject to SEC disclosure rules.

- Keep local issues local—try to keep your crisis from being the poster child for a national debate.

Today there's a larger arsenal of digital tools available in a crisis. But there's no substitute for being prepared.

COUNTERACTING SURPRISE THROUGH CRISIS PREPAREDNESS

You cannot fully eliminate the element of surprise in a crisis. Despite the inherent risks associated with chemicals, Magnablend was taken by surprise, as were the scores of other businesses that experience threatening emissions, leaks, and explosions every year. But being prepared for crisis will give your organization the ability to act with greater speed and agility and to buy precious time during an emergency. My team and I have helped prepare large multinational companies to deal with the unexpected.

The first action we take in a crisis preparedness assignment is to conduct a vulnerability analysis. We meet with the senior leadership team to identify emerging, existing, and potential issues that could require a crisis response and strategic communications. This process includes a review of all risks—hazardous chemicals, data breaches, product defects, employee misconduct, weather catastrophes, terrorism—whatever might threaten the company, its people, and its reputation. Then we prioritize the vulnerabilities, depending on the magnitude of the threat and the likelihood of it confronting the company.

You cannot fully eliminate the element of surprise in a crisis.

The next step is to develop a crisis plan for each major type of risk. This should take the form of a dynamic crisis playbook that outlines actions for various scenarios. The plan should:

- Establish a response team and define the roles;
- Create a response timeline;
- Create escalation protocols—objective criteria and thresholds that will trigger action under the crisis plan;
- Develop holding statements and FAQs that can be quickly augmented and deployed in the event of a crisis;
- Develop basic pre-approved talking points;
- Prepare pre-approved content for dark sites, social media, and other channels;
- Assemble key information about the company that will be necessary to use in crisis communications: location of facilities, their size, what they produce, how many employees, etc.

ISSUE RADAR DASHBOARD

OVERALL STATUS:
HIGH

ALL MENTIONS:
HIGH: 4,476

RED FLAGS:
MED: 443

INFLUENCER MENTIONS:
LOW: 464

WEBSITE HITS:
LOW: 2,334

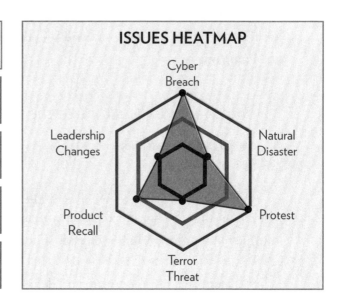

ISSUES HEATMAP

SITUATION: CYBER BREACH
STATUS HIGH

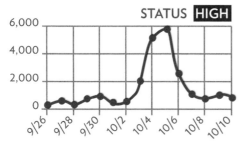

SITUATION: TERROR THREAT
STATUS LOW

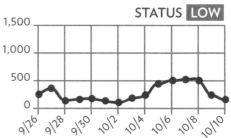

SITUATION: NATURAL DISASTER
STATUS LOW

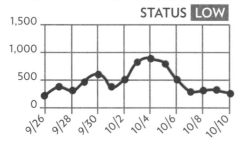

SITUATION: PROTEST
STATUS HIGH

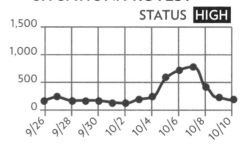

It's useful to create a graphic representation of the vulnerabilities—a dashboard that lists the risks, the seriousness of each, the current status, and the company's state of preparedness. Typically, we code each issue green, yellow, or red. Green signifies low or no threat or an issue that has been successfully managed. Yellow represents an elevated level of concern because there is a growing volume of media coverage and social media conversation, or increasing challenges posed by the threat, or perhaps a significant milestone or anniversary is soon to be reached that requires special vigilance. Red is the highest level of alert because of evidence of an imminent crisis or an emergency in progress. The dashboard and the monitoring process function as an issue radar, constantly sweeping the horizon.

In the digital era, a crisis often begins bubbling underground on social media before it rises to the surface in conventional media. We enlist sophisticated listening technology to detect, track, and analyze online conversations on each topic, resulting in regular reporting that informs the communications strategy. The issue management system—informed by the vulnerability analysis, the issue radar, and the listening updates—should become a routine agenda item at monthly meetings of senior management.

In the case of Tokyo Electric Power Company (TEPCO) and other clients, we have prepared daily and weekly listening and measurement reports so the company can stay abreast of the volume, tone, and sentiment of the conversation on digital media. Years after the March 2011 accident at the Fukushima Daiichi nuclear plant, that conversation continues as the cleanup effort proceeds, and spikes from time to time in response to developments there.

A WHITE HOUSE PERSPECTIVE

EARNING THE BENEFIT OF THE DOUBT

Dan Bartlett, Executive Vice President of
Corporate Affairs for Walmart

Dan Bartlett was a senior White House staff member serving President George W. Bush during the 9/11 and Hurricane Katrina crises. He is now Executive Vice President of Corporate Affairs at Walmart, responsible for corporate communications and government relations.

"It's interesting how much the news cycle times have changed since the Bush Administration," says Bartlett. "Trying to control a narrative from the White House is complex. It will always be unique, because it's the closest thing to free media that you're going to get. You don't have to pitch reporters. It's more about what you're going to say to whom. It's almost like a fulltime crisis exercise."

Smoke versus Fire

"What always has been my big issue in the early stage of a crisis is determining, 'Is this going to be smoke or fire?'" Bartlett explains that at Walmart, "We're trying to use data and technology, using bots and algorithms, to determine, based on a certain set of facts from the past, what is going on in the present. That is, can we predict which events will be fire and not smoke? Can we learn from pattern analysis in real time if there are factors that can tell us which events will accelerate exponentially on social media and therefore become a reputation and enterprise risk? Which ones can be tolerated and managed? We are in the early stages of figuring that out."

Throwing Out the Old Crisis Book

"After Hurricane Katrina we were dealing with a contested set of facts—the government's facts versus what the media was reporting. Of course, that's why you train in advance, so you're not making it up as you go.

"We executed a crisis book for a different kind of storm. We were prepared for a traditional storm that hits the coast of Florida. But how do you know when you have to throw the old crisis book out and *intentionally* start making it up as you go? Large, complex organizations over-rely on precedent. We're seeing now that because of digital [media], some of the things that worked in the past will not work in the future."

Developing Your Own Content

"Images are powerful, and the way they are now distributed makes them even more powerful. It's interesting how much the Trump administration is pushing the envelope in bypassing traditional media and using their own platforms to speak to supporters. Digital media lets us all reach the people we need to reach far more efficiently and at times, more effectively, than using traditional media in a crisis. It can give you much more control over the narrative. Of course, it can hurt you as much as help you if you don't use it properly. But the ability to generate your own content is a huge opportunity in a crisis. That's a game changer."

Earning the Benefit of the Doubt

"I talk to my team frequently about how most of the work on crisis should be in preparation," explains Bartlett. "What you're striving for is to get the benefit of the doubt from stakeholders, employees, the media, and the public. The only way you will get the benefit of the doubt is if they know something else about you—some sort of context to filter the event through. If you try to create that message in the middle of a crisis, it becomes very self-serving and obvious. The only way to effectively create the context is to make regular deposits to build your identity or your brand—almost like a bank account. You make deposits every month because you never know when that big withdrawal is going to come."

CONVERSATION ANALYSIS

VOLUME

Conversation volume spiked dramatically following the plant explosion. Influencer coverage was the major catalyst.

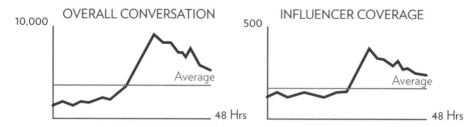

TOPIC BREAKDOWN

Talk of evacuation and travel disruptions dominated the conversation following the earthquake. After the plant explosion, conversation quickly shifted to discussion of fault/blame and criticism of the CEO's statement.

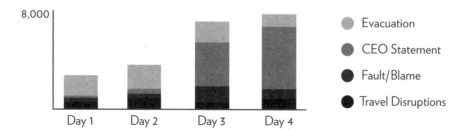

PLATFORM BREAKDOWN

Twitter remained the dominant channel in the conversation. Local news coverage and national media were the major drivers.

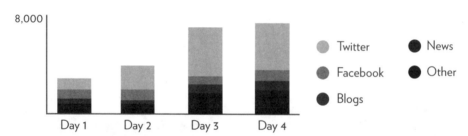

SOCIAL MEDIA INQUIRIES

Community managers have been inundated with inquiries on both Facebook and Twitter. Recommendation to increase staffing and to address common concerns/questions in a corporate blog post.

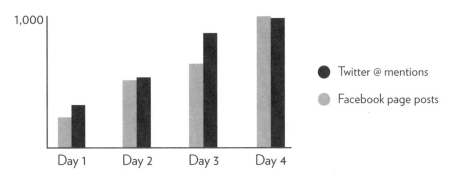

● Twitter @ mentions

● Facebook page posts

COMPETITOR SHARE OF VOICE

As expected, conversation volume was dramatically higher for Our Brand than our competitors. The CEO of Company X was alleged to have been critical of our safety standards. This should be monitored closely.

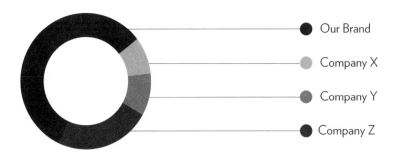

● Our Brand

● Company X

● Company Y

● Company Z

MENTION HIGHLIGHTS

News @OurBrand — Follow

CEO offers little clarity following major plant explosion.

↩ 21   ⟲ 800   ♥ 2,000

Media @OurBrand — Follow

Questions linger about steps taken to avoid devastating explosion.

↩ 21   ⟲ 800   ♥ 2,000

Mother @OurBrand — Follow

My son works at that plant. Please help me get in contact with him.

↩ 21   ⟲ 800   ♥ 2,000

What are we looking for through monitoring? We want to know what the public conversation is saying about your brand. In a previous era, we might do overnight polling. In the digital era, there is much to be learned through sophisticated listening.

- What is the communications volume in digital and conventional media?
- Is it escalating?
- How does it compare to typical volume?
- At what point does the volume justify a response?

We need to consider the communications channels that are involved.

- Is the issue contained on one channel?
- Where did the issue first surface?
- Who are the key influencers leading the conversation?
- Do we have relationships with them, and can we engage them?

Finally, we need to analyze the content of the conversations.

- What are the burning questions that need answers?
- What are the major arguments being advanced and are they accurate?
- What is the tone of the conversation?

YOUR VALUES SHOULD INFORM
CRISIS RESPONSE

It's very important that a company have a clear understanding of its culture before a crisis occurs. We recently led a crisis simulation at a major international corporation. Afterward, the CEO asked if I thought his decisions during the crisis lived up to the culture and the values of the company. So I asked, "What are your values?" He replied that the company aspired to put the customer's needs first and to provide the highest level of service. I had to say, "In that case, the answer is 'no.'" Because during the simulation, the company spent too much time playing defense and trying to protect its interests *before* telling its customers what was happening.

Many companies have not really examined their culture from the perspective of a crisis. If, in the middle of a crisis, you are asking yourself which of your values will inform your actions, then you are probably not managing the crisis well.

If you want to be authentic and transparent in a crisis—assuming that is your objective—then you need to be committed to those values in advance. Your executive team, your legal team, and your communications team need to understand that your actions must uphold those values. Deciding in advance which values are paramount in crisis will aid your speed and agility.

Another factor to consider: What is the net perception of your company that you want your constituents to have in the aftermath of a crisis? Do you want your stakeholders to regard your organization as forthcoming, authentic, responsible—or something else?

Before you can focus on crisis preparedness, you need to focus on your cultural identity. That identity and the values that exemplify it will inform your response to crisis.

SIMULATION IMPROVES READINESS

A full-scale crisis simulation is invaluable because it tests plans, systems, and people.

The goal is not to predict and prepare for a highly specific crisis. But a well-constructed simulation will test communications systems, emergency equipment, and facilities. Moreover, it exposes vulnerabilities and provides a window into how people function under pressure. Simulations involve decision-making, tight deadlines, incomplete information, personality conflicts, and interdepartmental friction. Under the pressure of making decisions, leaders emerge. In some cases, the process may reveal personal weaknesses and discomfort in people as well as flaws in systems and facilities. At one recent simulation I conducted, participants were shocked to discover that the conference space that had been designated as the situation room did not have a wireless communications signal.

For one global client, we created a crisis simulation of a major cyber breach at its headquarters. We had approximately 50 management and communications executives in three offices in North America participating in a simulation designed to compress two simulated days into a four-hour drill. The management team was required to respond to a cascade of more than 30 developments over the course of the simulation. Especially in the case of financial organizations, the probability of experiencing a security breach is extremely high.

A FULL-SCALE CRISIS SIMULATION IS INVALUABLE BECAUSE IT TESTS PLANS, SYSTEMS, AND PEOPLE.

Executing a crisis plan—even in simulation—can be invaluable when hackers strike.

We also helped enhance preparedness for an island nation in the Caribbean that had experienced two tourism crises in its recent past. My team and I conducted a simulation of an explosion that threatened the entire energy infrastructure of the island. We prepared mock Facebook and Twitter posts, articles from Caribbean media, traveler inquiries to the island's tourism authority, a YouTube video, NBC, ABC, and CNN reports, a Greenpeace editorial, and other news outlet reporting for the crisis team to contend with. This exercise was arduous for the client, but the island became much better prepared for the next emergency as a result of its willingness to thoroughly simulate a crisis.

Simulation participants will often complain that they are being presented with a parade of compounding disasters that is too far-fetched. But they are wrong. We conducted a simulation for the ATP Tennis Tour in which we introduced a racial incident at the US Open, a gambling scandal, and a player testing positive for a perfor-mance-enhancing drug. While the tour officials were complimentary about the experience, they said that it seemed improbable that the tour would have to face three such severe challenges at the same time. But within about a year, there was a racial incident at the US Open, a gambling scandal involving a prominent player on the tour, and positive tests for performance-enhancing drugs of several tour players. Indeed, one of the key lessons being learned around the world from the Fukushima disaster is that we must be more imagina-tive in anticipating how many different ways things can go wrong and how small individual failures can cascade into a catastrophe.

ESTABLISHING A COMMAND CENTER

In a crisis, you will need a command center or situation room. All major organizations should have a physical space prepared well in advance for responding to an emergency. It needs to be big enough to accommodate the crisis management team and support staff. Other requirements include:

- Access to live TV;
- Video conferencing capability;
- Access to social media listening;
- Flip charts/white boards;

- Food and beverage service;
- Publishing capability for all social media platforms;
- Multiple phone lines;
- Fast, secure wifi;
- Listening data visualization;
- Printer access.

This facility need not sit idle waiting for the crisis that may never come. Its capabilities can and should be used to enhance issue monitoring and management during "normal" times and should also be used to conduct any simulations.

Finally, while many crises last for days, some extend over long periods of time. You may need to consider deploying fresh team members during a long-term crisis, because people can experience burnout or adopt a highly defensive communications outlook. If your team begins to develop an attitude of "it's us against the world" or "the media is out to get us," your communications will suffer. It's time to bring in reinforcements with a more positive attitude.

We must be more imaginative in anticipating how many different ways things can go wrong and how small individual failures can cascade into a catastrophe.

BUILDING THE CONNECTED COMMAND CENTER

1. Access to live TV
2. Video conferencing capability
3. Access to social media listening
4. Flip charts / white boards
5. Food and beverage service

6. Publishing capability for all social media platforms
7. Multiple phone lines
8. Fast, secure wifi
9. Listening data visualization
10. Printer access

DEVELOPING YOUR OWN OUTLET FOR NEWS

In a crisis, your constituents are going to want information, and they're going to want it fast. Moreover, you are competing with every other media outlet to tell the story. You can become *the* source of news of the situation by communicating early and often. If you don't fill the information vacuum, someone else will. So we want to shape and define the narrative without appearing adversarial or reactive. Through speed, agility, and authenticity of your communications, you can help build public confidence in your organization. Because you own the situation and much of the information, you can break your own news on social media and on websites you control.

A valuable way to achieve this is to develop a standby dark site—a website that is populated with useful content about your organization and its operations that remains unpublished until a crisis occurs. This will provide a communications outlet for the crisis where customers, employees, neighbors, regulators, and the media can go to get relevant information, which should include rich media such as video, photos, maps, and infographics.

If, for example, the risk involves a data breach, then the dark site might include frequently asked questions about what customers can do to protect themselves, information about the ongoing efforts of

You can become the source of news of the situation by communicating early and often. If you don't fill the information vacuum, someone else will.

the company to provide IT security, and evergreen content about the company and its history in dealing with threats to cyber security. The site should be designed to provide a real-time news section for the latest developments in the crisis. You will need these digital tools in an emergency, and it will take time to develop them, so why not have them ready in advance? When crisis occurs, having these assets ready will help you fill the information vacuum by publishing the site with the flip of a switch.

TAKEAWAYS

- ☐ **Identify vulnerabilities** and develop an issue radar system.

- ☐ **Have a crisis plan** and test it regularly.

- ☐ **Establish a situation room.** Isolate the crisis management team from routine responsibilities.

- ☐ **Get all the information you can,** but don't succumb to inaction. You'll never have *all* the facts as a crisis unfolds.

- ☐ **Leverage your advocates**—both internal and external.

- ☐ **Use social media** to break your own news.

- ☐ **Develop a separate digital platform** from the company's main website that can be deployed if necessary.

INSUFFICIENT INFORMATION

You can't know everything, but share what you do.

3

SUDDENLY YOU'RE A YOUTUBE SENSATION

"When written in Chinese, the word for crisis is composed of two characters. One represents danger, and the other represents opportunity."
—*President John F. Kennedy*

On April 20, 2010, the Macondo oil well, far below the surface of the Gulf of Mexico, shot methane gas up through a mile of pipe to the drilling platform of the *Deepwater Horizon*. The 320-foot-tall semi-submersible rig began to tremble. An unfamiliar hissing sound was heard by the crew. And then, amidst the thousands of tons of floating machinery in operation, the gas found an ignition source. The rig exploded, sending a plume of fire toward the sky that was easily visible to satellites 22,000 miles above. Fire and debris roared through the vessel. The lives of 126 crew members were in peril. It was everything the survivors could do to evacuate, hauling injured crew into life boats and rafts. With flames at their heels, some crew members leaped, falling a distance equal to a seven-story building and into the oily black water below.

Eleven members of the crew were never found. The Deepwater Horizon sank two days later. Soon an enormous oil slick appeared that would be the precursor to a leak that would release five million barrels of oil into the Gulf over the course of 87 days.

It became the world's largest accidental oil spill and a crisis on a scale rarely seen.

British Petroleum (BP) was in the "insufficient information" stage of crisis. No one knew exactly what had happened, who was in charge, or what to do next. BP employees could not see the well at the floor of the Gulf, and the equipment critical to getting answers was a mile beneath the sea. Even the members of the crew who were on deck at the time of the explosion could not explain what had happened. From that moment on, all decisions would be made in the glare of global public scrutiny. Despite a crew member's attempt to activate the well's massive blowout preventer prior to evacuation, the fire raged on. It appeared that the fire was still being fueled by the vast reservoir of oil that had enticed BP to drill there. The well should have been sealed, but it was beginning to become apparent that the blowout preventer had failed.

BP had reached stage two of crisis, insufficient information, with a long list of questions:

- Who was responsible for the explosion?

- What exactly had happened?

- What was the extent of the human casualties?

- How much oil was being released?

- When and how would the well be sealed?

- How great were the environmental damages?

- How great were the economic damages?

As the crisis wore on into May, BP realized that it was losing the battle in the court of public opinion. Despite trying to frame the accident as a product of Transocean, the owner of the rig, the public viewed the mess as BP's problem. BP then decided to release video of the leak. One clip showed oil and gas escaping from the well and another showed a botched attempt to seal the leak with a containment dome. BP then got an earful from the public and elected officials, who realized that if there was a video cam providing the company with round-the-clock images, and the government was spending billions trying to help BP fix the leak, then everyone should be able to watch. BP released the real-time video, which became known as "Spillcam." Every news report about the spill could cut to the Spillcam footage. Moveover, scientists could now analyze the video and make their own estimates about the size of the leak. Several university professors calculated that BP's calculations were underestimating the spill volume by more than 1,000 percent.

The BP saga was long and frustrating. Some of the challenges were of unprecedented scale. But it was entirely predictable that a major blowout could occur, and BP's performance conveyed arrogance, confusion, and incompetence. Weak communications compounded the problems BP faced and helped to alienate the company from stakeholders who shared the goal of controlling the blowout and protecting the environment.

To catalog just a few of the mistakes that BP made:

- Early speculation by BP was based on overly favorable estimates about activity at the bottom of the ocean without hard data. BP could have used the full range of estimates—from best- to worst-case scenarios—and been candid about what it didn't know.

- BP CEO Tony Hayward offered speculation that minimized the environmental impact of the spill and ignored evidence to the contrary.

- BP positioned the crisis as the rig owner's fault—"It wasn't our accident . . ."—which gave the appearance that BP executives were blaming others and minimizing the energy company's role in the tragedy.

- Statements by BP were slow, uninformative, and confusing— replete with legal jargon instead of plain language.

- CEO Hayward made multiple mistakes that would portray him as unreliable, indecisive, tone-deaf, and perhaps most memorably, terribly self-centered when he lamented to the media, "I want my life back."

Blaming others is rarely a successful strategy. It didn't work during the tire recall of 2000–2001, when Ford was forced to recall cars it had sold with defective Firestone tires. The early part of that crisis included disagreements, accusations, and litigation between multiple parties concerning who was responsible for the dangerous tire failures and rollover problems with the Ford Explorer that resulted in scores of fatalities. Ultimately the dispute tarnished both companies and led to the disintegration of a 100-year business relationship between Ford and Firestone. Years later, when I was involved in the Dell laptop battery recall, the Dell management team decided that even though the defective batteries were made by Sony, Dell would own the problem. Sony bore most of the cost of the recall, but Dell accepted responsibility and took the lead in solving the problem.

BLAMING OTHERS IS RARELY A SUCCESSFUL STRATEGY.

INSUFFICIENT INFORMATION DOESN'T MEAN INACTION

In this chapter, I want to demonstrate that there are strategies for dealing with insufficient information that can address the concerns of stakeholders, keep the public informed, and protect your organization's reputation.

In the early stages of crisis, there are more questions than answers. It's important to resist the temptation to postpone communications until all the facts have been established. As I said previously, crisis creates a vacuum. The question is, do you want the vacuum filled with speculation, innuendo, sensationalism, or your adversaries' key messages? If not, you must create content to fill the communications channels that are important to you, because otherwise, the vacuum will be filled by someone else.

While this stage of crisis may be characterized by a lack of information, it's the time to make the most of the information that you do possess. The standby website that I described in the previous chapter should be activated, containing relevant information about the company, its operations, its emergency response protocols, and links to reputable news sources. This is also the time to leverage whatever news you control. You can publish updates on the crisis on your website, post video with news or background information, or present charts or illustrations that provide insights to audiences and to the media that are hungry for information.

MAKE THE MOST OF THE INFORMATION THAT YOU DO POSSESS.

LEGAL LIABILITY VERSUS SPEED AND AGILITY

Another complicating factor in the insufficient information stage is that of potential legal liability and sometimes also the potential for criminal prosecution. Lawyers are responsible for minimizing the risks of both. During the early stages of a crisis, when the facts are elusive and the risk of a potentially crippling admission of negligence or wrongdoing is high, the legal team will advise saying as little as possible. But in the situation room, there needs to be an equally assertive and articulate advocate to speak on behalf of defending the company's reputation and brand. BP famously described the Deepwater Horizon explosion as "a complex and inter-linked series of mechanical failures, human judgments, engineering design, operational implementation and team interfaces." Legalistic language such as that may have passed muster in the legal department, but it does nothing for regaining public trust.

In companies with a strong engineering culture, there is a similar reluctance to communicate without conclusive data. Engineers are accustomed to basing decisions on a complete understanding of the facts and specifications. For most things engineers do, that is a desirable, even essential trait. But in a crisis, it can make a company seem unresponsive, secretive, and untrustworthy. It is possible, and often necessary, to share limited information while acknowledging that much remains to be learned about a situation.

In many cases, process can be your ally. The mere act of telling people what you're going to do to discover what actually happened and the process you're going to follow to find answers will help fill

There needs to be an equally assertive and articulate advocate to speak on behalf of defending the company's reputation and brand.

the vacuum. If it's communicated thoroughly with the proper voice, it can convey genuine authenticity and transparency.

During the last four decades of the 20th century, the name Red Adair was identified with slaying the world's biggest oil well fires. A World War II bomb squad veteran with a history of extinguishing more than 2,000 oilfield fires, Adair was known throughout the world as the man to call if you had a fire that no one else could handle. John Wayne even played a character based on Adair in the 1968 film *Hellfighters* (It should be noted that Adair never tackled a giant blowout a mile beneath the sea).

Based on his reputation as a troubleshooter, a company with an oil-fueled inferno could accomplish a lot by merely telling the public that Red Adair was on his way. It created the perception that things were being handled and the process of recovery was underway. Red Adair would take care of it.

There are many ways you can create a "Red Adair moment" that helps you turn the corner in the early stages of a crisis. A blue-ribbon panel can be appointed. A special investigator can be named. An independent, third-party review can be commissioned. The right expert will inspire public confidence and demonstrate your commitment to discovering the facts, fixing the problems, and learning valuable lessons from the experience.

THE RED ADAIR MOMENT

My team and I worked on the aftermath of the Penn State University scandal involving criminal charges of child sex abuse by former football coach Jerry Sandusky, and related civil litigation. After Penn State's board of regents fired or accepted resignations from the university's president, head football coach, and several other officials, the situation cried out for an independent review. The board hired Louis Freeh, the former director of the FBI and a former federal judge, to determine what had occurred and recommend a path forward. Freeh, with his exalted reputation, was Penn State's version of Red Adair at the time. I certainly don't want to minimize the conflict, litigation, and criminal prosecutions that have occurred since the release of what has become known as the "Freeh Report," but Freeh's independence, experience, and reputation for integrity gave Penn State some time and stability to work through the crisis.

It should be noted that many loyal Joe Paterno partisans believe Freeh unfairly judged Coach Paterno's role in the scandal. They draw unfavorable comparisons to the rush to judgment in the case against Richard Jewell, who was wrongly suspected of the 1996 Atlanta Olympic bombing while Freeh was FBI director. Jewell was later exonerated.

Another tragic example from a college campus, albeit a very different situation, demonstrates some of the principles for dealing with insufficient information.

In April, 2016, the body of a young female was found in a creek on the campus of The University of Texas at Austin (UT). Social and conventional media reported the event, but for several news cycles there was little confirmed information to share, such as the victim's identity, whether she was a student, or if criminal activity was suspected. The victim was a young woman who was possibly a student, and there was understandable alarm and anxiety throughout the university community.

The university, through its president, Gregory Fenves, communicated early and often to keep the campus informed. He told the community what officials knew and what they didn't know, and he did so using multiple social media platforms as well as conventional media. While the early messages contained very little information, President Fenves expressed concern with a personal and familial tone.

Ultimately, it was determined that an 18-year-old first-year dance student from Portland, Oregon was the victim in what was the first homicide on campus in nearly 50 years. It was a horrific situation, but the university took action in ways that exemplify good crisis management.

- UT worked closely with the family of the victim to be sensitive to its needs and to forward messages from the family to the campus community.

- UT worked diligently with multiple law enforcement and other agencies to help apprehend a suspect and implement additional safety measures on campus.

- President Fenves commissioned an independent review of campus safety procedures.

- UT attended to the needs of students and the campus with extensive counseling services, and it created a path for healing with a memorial service, a dance performance in memory of the victim, and a memorial fund.

- Finally, President Fenves created the expectation that something positive would come out of the tragedy through enhanced safety awareness and expanded security measures on campus.

On the whole, the university's actions demonstrated:

Authenticity—Fenves at times spoke as a father of two daughters;

Transparency—telling what it knew and what it didn't know;

Speed—quickly joining forces with other public safety agencies and alerting the campus;

Agility—sharing information with the community promptly;

Creativity—establishing ways to honor the victim and to express grief through a public memorial service and through the arts and by creating enduring positive change.

A few days after the crime, a troubled 17-year-old runaway from a foster home was charged with murder in the case.

A LEGAL PERSPECTIVE

BALANCING COMMUNICATIONS AND THE LAW

Marcy Wilder, Partner and Director, Privacy and Cybersecurity Practice at Hogan Lovells

---

Cyberattacks are increasingly common and pose a broad range of risks to victims. Specialized legal counsel is often required to clean up the resulting legal and regulatory mess.

Marcy Wilder, a partner in the Washington, DC, office of Hogan Lovells, represents organizations coping with large and complex cyberattacks and privacy investigations. She is former deputy general counsel of the US Department of Health and Human Services, where she led the legal team that drafted the HIPAA health and privacy regulations.

There is a natural tension between lawyers and communication specialists in crisis response. "Lawyers are focused on legal issues and the potential liability, and the communications professionals are focused how to tell the story. But in the end, both should be focused on how to provide a truthful and accurate account. Only through a balanced approach can you reach an understanding of what is really in the best interests of the victims and the affected company," says Wilder, who runs her firm's global privacy and cybersecurity practice.

What Do You Really Know?

"In the beginning it's really hard to quantify the legal and the reputational risks," says Wilder. "When you're in the middle of a crisis, you often don't yet know what's happened, and that makes it quite challenging when you need to make a public statement. My experience is that in an effort to shape the story, the communications team has a tendency to want to tell more than what we actually know. The lawyers' job in that case is to look hard and realistically at the facts we have, let the communications professionals shape how those facts are described and disclosed, but help the team determine what we actually know and not get out ahead of the story."

Cyber Attacks and the Law

"Oftentimes in a cyberattack," says Wilder, "a specific set of laws and legal considerations are at play, so you're not just dealing with the basics of crisis management—you've got to consider breach notification laws and obligations to government regulators. The specific set of laws at play will depend in part on the type of cyberattack and the sector affected. For example, health care breaches bring into play a specific set of privacy obligations that apply only to health data. Early on in a cyber crisis there are extremely important and time-sensitive roles for forensics, legal, and communications in terms of the kinds of actions that need to be taken. These include preserving records and evidence, engaging the right kinds of experts, and establishing the role of attorney-client privilege.

"When cybercrime is involved, I look at the effect on the individuals impacted, the effect on the institution that has been attacked, and the actions the company is taking to protect those at risk. In cases where credit card numbers or social security numbers have been compromised, there are specific steps that can be taken to protect individuals, often involving credit monitoring and identity theft protection. Where a breach involves personal medical or other sensitive data and the risk is reputational, sometimes there is not much that can be done to protect individuals after the fact. The focus needs to be on preventing these kinds of attacks in the first place.

"Who bears responsibility for prevention? There's a role for companies and a role for government. Companies need a coordinated, mature, and appropriately resourced information security program. Lawmakers and law enforcement should be focused more on cyber-defense and prosecuting cyber criminals instead of the victims. Sometimes companies are victimized first by a cyberattack and then again by government regulators and prosecutors. That is not a healthy dynamic, in part, because it discourages the types of reporting and cooperation that can prevent cyber incidents in the first place."

Cybercrime Stages

Wilder describes three distinct stages of cyberattack response:

Stage 1: "At this point we've got to figure out what happened and make sure it's not still happening. There's a lot of work initially for the IT department and forensics experts. Is the attacker still in our system? If so, how do we get them out and assure that they can't get back in? Was data accessed or exfiltrated? In the case of ransomware, you're also trying to figure out if and how the encrypted data can be recovered and if the environment is secure."

Stage 2: "You now have some sense of what happened, and you are assessing the damage and how best to communicate with those affected, with law enforcement, and with regulators, while ensuring you are meeting any applicable breach notification requirements."

Stage 3: "In this stage the focus is on further securing the environment against future attacks, dealing with regulators, and lawsuits that have been threatened or filed. If we've done our job well, we've anticipated the kind of legal claims that will be presented and helped drive the process in a way that protects the company and puts it in the best position to face government investigations and lawsuits."

Practice, Practice, Practice

What should companies be doing to prepare? "There are two steps that those who have been through a cyberattack say are a tremendous help in minimizing data loss, pre-empting fines and lawsuits, and avoiding costly customer backlash. First, have a good comprehensive incident-response plan. Many companies have an incident-response plan developed by the IT department or a breach response communications plan. Those cannot serve as an enterprise-wide incident-response plan. You need a comprehensive response plan that involves all the people who will be involved—the executive team, IT, HR, legal, communications, and the units with customer-facing employees. They all need to know they are part of the response team. In a crisis, you need to know who's on the team and what their job is. After you have a plan, the best thing you can do is practice. It's hard to convince people that devoting a half-day to a table-top simulation is worthwhile, but there's nothing more valuable for crisis preparedness."

Wilder adds, "Companies that have practiced and then experienced a cyberattack, are *always* glad they practiced."

THE POWER OF NARRATIVE

This is also the time to begin to think about the narrative of the events and the role in that narrative that your organization will play. If you can't envision how your company will be cast in a drama, you are limited in your ability to change or strengthen that role. I have lived all over the world and operated in many different cultures, and I have discovered that storytelling is universal. People want to interpret events in terms of villain, victim, hero, and moral. You must ask, what is the net impact you are trying to achieve through your communications? Which of those roles does your organization play in the story that is being told? How do you want to be perceived? How will external audiences view your role in the crisis? It may seem premature to begin to focus on narrative when you don't have all the facts, but there are times when an envisioned narrative arc can help inform strategy. I'll share some examples to illustrate this point. But it's important to emphasize that to be effective, the narrative must be grounded in fact. You can't just make it up.

Stories stand out from the daily barrage of information every person is subjected to every day. If you think about your day and your daily exposure to media, you realize that we are all saturated by more information than we can possibly absorb: the Internet, television, radio, newspapers, email, Facebook, Twitter, news feeds, blogs, Instagram, and many other forms of digital distraction. All that information competes for everyone's attention. Your message must stand out to earn an audience. The goal is to create content so strong that people want to share it with their friends.

Good stories don't just convey information. They create an

CREATE CONTENT SO STRONG THAT PEOPLE WANT TO SHARE IT WITH THEIR FRIENDS.

ELEMENTS OF A COMPELLING STORY

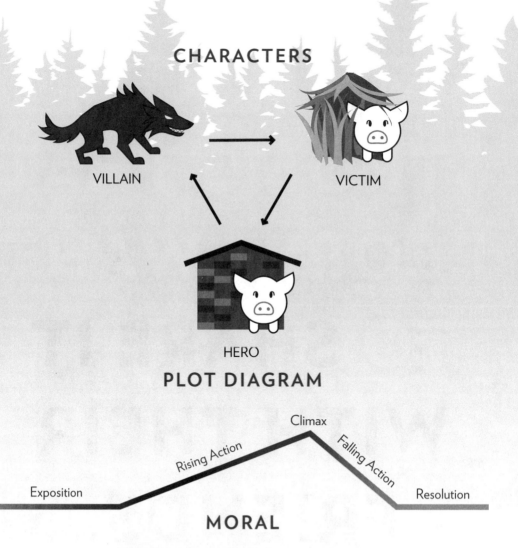

CHARACTERS

VILLAIN

VICTIM

HERO

PLOT DIAGRAM

Climax

Rising Action

Falling Action

Exposition

Resolution

MORAL

BUILD A HOUSE OF BRICKS

NET IMPACT

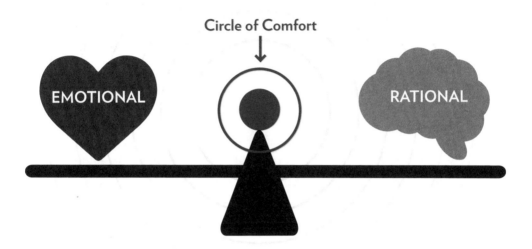

Circle of Comfort

EMOTIONAL

RATIONAL

FRAMEWORK FOR COMPELLING MESSAGING

In addition to net impact, compelling messaging is frequently driven by the ability to demonstrate credibility, show empathy and apply expertise.

1. Demonstrate Credibility by sharing accurate information that positions you as an authoritative source and makes your story relevant to the audience.

2. Show Empathy by demonstrating an understanding of what key constituents need most during the crisis.

3. Apply Expertise by taking action to proactively address the problem or concern.

emotional connection that allows members of the audience to integrate their own ideas and experiences with the story. Emotionally charged stories can even trigger the release of neurotransmitters that regulate pleasure and can improve memory and recall. "The best stories lead from the heart, not the mind," says Stacey Snider, co-chair of 20th Century Fox. A narrative packaged in story form has sticking power because stories are more memorable than facts. That's why people in memory competitions, memory athletes, translate abstract numbers into stories with strong visual images. Creating these "memory palaces" aids retention. Stories stand out. Stories invite retelling.

Stories can change the way our brains work and have the potential to change brain chemistry. An exciting story can increase heart rate and respiration, and stress hormones can be released. Furthermore, audience members may experience empathy for the characters and begin to feel what the characters are feeling. Authentic stories can be used to illustrate your organization's values and culture and to celebrate your people. But in order to achieve this, stories must be based on actions that exemplify the values of your organization and its culture.

THE BEST STORIES LEAD FROM THE HEART, NOT THE MIND.

YOUR BRAIN ON STORIES

Mirroring
Listeners experience similar brain activity to each other and the speaker.

Dopamine
Emotionally-charged stories release dopamine, which improves memory and recall accuracy.

Neural Coupling
User turns story into their own ideas and experiences.

Cortex Activity
Processing facts activates two areas of the brain. Stories can engage many additional areas.

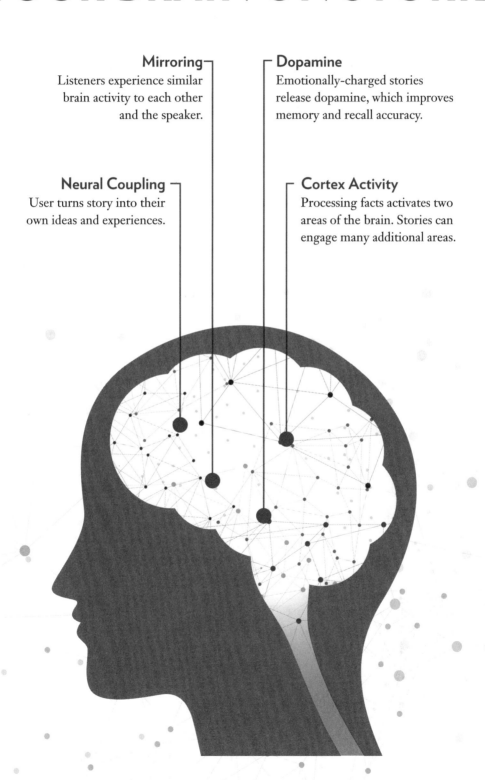

My team and I continue to help TEPCO (Tokyo Electric Power Company) with its communications and reputation management in the aftermath of the Great East Japan Earthquake, which caused the tsunami and nuclear meltdowns in Fukushima in 2011. While I will have more to say about that crisis in a later chapter, we encountered a situation where TEPCO was initially cast as the villain. After all, its nuclear plant failed and contaminated the region, forcing thousands of people from their homes. Because the earthquake had a magnitude of 9.0, the largest in Japan's recorded history, it caused waves three times as high as the power plants had been designed to withstand. The tidal wave would overwhelm cooling systems and reactor buildings.

But through working hard to earn the public's trust, to be authentic and transparent, and to demonstrate a strong commitment to restoring Fukushima, TEPCO has shifted some of those initial perceptions. Many people in Japan have come to view the tsunami as the villain. As more people began to understand the narrative of the human response to this unprecedented earthquake, a group of workers known as the Fukushima 50 began to be cast as heroes. At great personal risk, these employees worked through aftershocks, flooding, radiation, power losses, and the lack of information about the fate of their families to prevent a much greater catastrophe. And other TEPCO workers, under inspired and creative leadership, made a Herculean effort to protect a second TEPCO nuclear facility, Fukushima Daini, from failure by jury-rigging an electrical connection that preserved the ability to cool that facility's reactor cores.

Now, years after the crisis, TEPCO is viewed by many in Japan as another victim of the earthquake—not an entirely blameless one, but

TOP 10 EARTHQUAKES WORLDWIDE

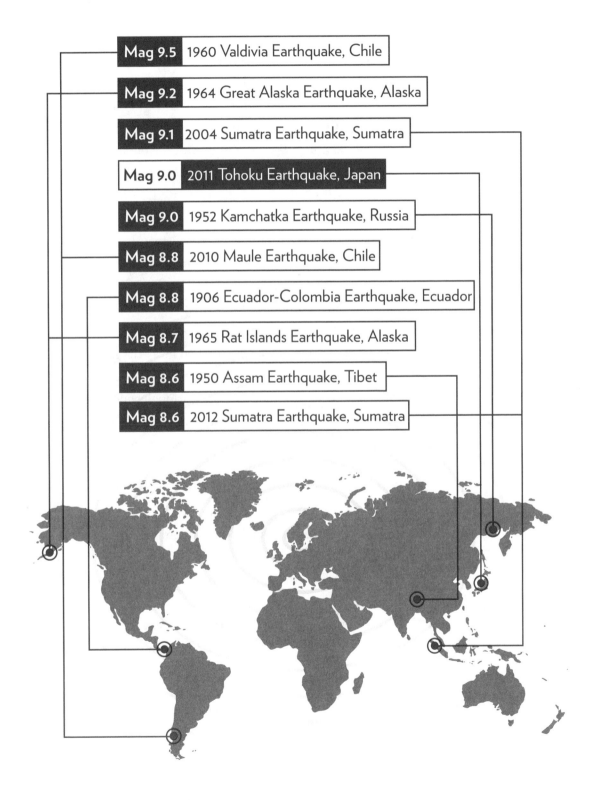

Mag 9.5 | 1960 Valdivia Earthquake, Chile

Mag 9.2 | 1964 Great Alaska Earthquake, Alaska

Mag 9.1 | 2004 Sumatra Earthquake, Sumatra

Mag 9.0 | 2011 Tohoku Earthquake, Japan

Mag 9.0 | 1952 Kamchatka Earthquake, Russia

Mag 8.8 | 2010 Maule Earthquake, Chile

Mag 8.8 | 1906 Ecuador-Colombia Earthquake, Ecuador

Mag 8.7 | 1965 Rat Islands Earthquake, Alaska

Mag 8.6 | 1950 Assam Earthquake, Tibet

Mag 8.6 | 2012 Sumatra Earthquake, Sumatra

a victim nonetheless. The villain was the earthquake and the tsunami. And what is the moral? Overconfidence and complacency must always be guarded against, and we must try harder to anticipate and prepare for the unexpected. TEPCO still has a lot of work to do, but it has gone a long way toward rebuilding its relationship with the public.

A recent article in *The New York Times Magazine* about Ben Rhodes, a fiction writer who has served throughout the Obama administration as deputy national security advisor, alludes to the powerful role of narrative in foreign policy: "Like Obama, Rhodes is a storyteller who uses a writer's tools to advance an agenda that is packaged as politics but is often quite personal. He is adept at constructing overarching plotlines with heroes and villains . . . He is the master shaper and retailer of Obama's foreign-policy narratives, at a time when the killer wave of social media has washed away the sand castles of the traditional press."

Another way of saying this is that raw facts and rational evidence may not be enough to get the job done. But a strong narrative with inherent emotional appeal, supported by facts and rational argument, is much more likely to prevail.

Storytelling is especially powerful with Millennials. They have a fundamental mistrust of institutions and a greater trust in peer-to-peer communications. Social media has allowed Millennials to create and share information with networks that give friends a strong sense of engagement and of participating in people's lives on an hour-by-hour or minute-by-minute basis. That's a powerful form of intimacy. Now technology has enabled intimacy between people and organizations on a much larger scale. A lot of organizations

A strong narrative with inherent emotional appeal, supported by facts and rational argument, is much more likely to prevail.

invest in digital technology to take advantage of scaled intimacy without creating the kind of engagement that only comes from *two-way* communication.

Millennials don't want to be talked at. They prefer to engage in conversation with brands and companies. In this dynamic, digital media provide two-way communication. You're offering valuable information to your stakeholders and customers. Ideally, great storytelling is one way you connect with them. Meanwhile Millennials and others tell you what they think, share comments and content, and perhaps become your advocates or brand ambassadors.

Three decades ago, we quantified customer satisfaction, and if your customers reported high levels of satisfaction, that was interpreted as successful engagement. Then the emphasis shifted from customer satisfaction to customer loyalty. This trend was exemplified in the influential 1996 business book, *The Loyalty Effect* by Frederick Reichheld. Research showed that superior customer satisfaction resulted in greater loyalty, which in turn generated higher profits and faster growth.

Later it was recognized that while it was highly desirable for customers to be satisfied and even more so to have earned their loyalty, a still higher form of allegiance was for customers to promote a brand to their friends, so "net promoter" scores became the rage.

A BURNING PLATFORM

One celebrated example of the power of storytelling is Nokia's 2011 burning platform memo.

The CEO of Nokia, Stephen Elop, wanted to make a dramatic statement that would herald a change in the culture of the company. He told the story of "a man who was working on an oil platform in the North Sea. He woke up one night from a loud explosion, which suddenly set his entire oil platform on fire. In mere moments, he was surrounded by flames. Through the smoke and heat, he barely made his way out of the chaos to the platform's edge. When he looked down over the edge, all he could see were the dark, cold, foreboding Atlantic waters."

As the fire approached him, the man had mere seconds to react. He could stand on the platform, and inevitably be consumed by the burning flames. Or, he could plunge 30 meters in to the freezing waters. The man was standing upon a "burning platform," and he needed to make a choice.

The man decided to jump, even though under normal conditions, he would never consider doing it. "But his platform was on fire." He survived the fall and the freezing water. He realized that only the burning platform could radically change his perspective.

"We too, are standing on a 'burning platform,'" said Elop, "and we must decide how we are going to change our behavior."

The memo went on to describe the disruption to the smart phone market caused by Apple and Android and the catastrophic effect on Nokia's market share. Through engaging storytelling, Elop got the attention not only of his employees, but of the entire business world.

Articles reporting the memo appeared in *The Wall Street Journal* and many other publications around the world.

> "We are working on a path forward—a path to rebuild our market leadership. . . . But, I believe that together, we can face the challenges ahead of us. Together, we can choose to define our future."

Nokia escaped the burning platform, although it needed help. Elop was the architect of the 2014 sale of Nokia to Microsoft for $7.2 billion.

THE ERA OF ENGAGEMENT

We are now in the era of engagement. The highest expression of customer engagement is the mutual exchange of value—you provide the customer with an exceptional experience and the customer promotes your brand in his or her social networks, or engages in a dialogue with you about how to make the customer experience even better. Or, as the next example illustrates, the customer uses digital tools to help you create or refine the product or service that will best meet his or her needs.

In 2005, our client, Dell Computer, was experiencing consumer complaints resulting from exponential growth and the relocation of customer support call centers from the United States to India. This was occurring as Dell was expanding its market share among customers who were less familiar with technology than its early

THE HIGHEST EXPRESSION OF CUSTOMER ENGAGEMENT IS THE MUTUAL EXCHANGE OF VALUE.

customer base. In addition to the customer service challenges, Dell was getting ready to conduct the largest safety recall in the history of the consumer electronics industry. The recall would include 4.1 million notebook computers with batteries that could, and at times did, erupt in flames.

This was the early stage of digital media, and Dell maintained a "look but don't touch" attitude toward bloggers. The company was not doing much online listening and even less responding to the conversation. One influential blogger and journalist, Jeff Jarvis, wrote a blog post called "Dell Hell" about his frustrating customer experience trying to obtain some technical support. One Jarvis post bore the headline, "Dell Lies. Dell Sucks."

Despite a great deal of online complaining about customer service problems, Jarvis could not get his computer service issues resolved.

As Jarvis would describe in *The Guardian* in 2005, "I decided to turn this into a test: Was Dell reading blogs? Would Dell respond to me in our public forum? Would it recognize the PR [crisis] that was brewing? Simple answer: No. Dell was silent. Dell failed the test. I emailed its marketing department: Anybody home? Anybody blogging? Nothing."

It took a few months, but my team and I persuaded the leadership at Dell that blogs like Jarvis's *BuzzMachine* had earned a great deal of respect and authority in the consumer marketplace. Paul Walker, who has been a friend and colleague over the years, kept calling me, saying, "Dell is getting killed online and you need a strategy." I brought Paul in as a consultant because he understood the power of the online conversation on brands very early in the digital era. Together, we helped Dell create its first social media strategy and its first blog. The battery recall was coming up. We had about two weeks' notice. So we did an audit of best practices in product recalls both within and outside the electronics industry. We used the key findings to inform a strategy. Then we created a mock *Harvard Business Review* article on how Dell got the recall right, which we shared with the executive team. We call this vision casting, which is to say, we try to determine what the most favorable outcome would look like, and then we create a strategy to achieve it.

To explain the recall and the battery problems, we had a senior Dell executive appear as a guest on *Squawk Box*, the CNBC news show that covers Wall Street. And Michael Dell said he wanted a listening forum that would "drain the swamp." That is, Dell wanted to directly engage with customers, understand their complaints, and fix the problems. Michael Dell came up with the idea of creating a crowdsourcing platform, which we helped design and implement, called IdeaStorm. The novel website gave customers a chance to submit ideas for improving products and customer service—and to just talk to someone at Dell. It also gave customers a chance to rate the ideas and ranked them in real-time so that everyone could see how the community responded. The headline for the site is "IdeaStorm can help take your idea and turn it into reality."

IdeaStorm not only served as a pressure release valve for customers' angst, but it also generated hundreds of ideas that Dell could implement. Developing backlit monitors was proposed by IdeaStorm, as was offering a Linux open source software platform.

Furthermore, IdeaStorm positioned Dell as a progressive company that listened to its customers.

Jarvis later wrote on his blog: "Dell realized that engaging in the conversation wasn't just a way to stop blogging customers like me from harming the brand. We, the customers, bring them great value besides our money: We alert them to problems. We will tell them what products we want. We share our knowledge about their products. We help fellow customers solve problems. We will sell their products. But this happens only if you have a decent product and service and only if you listen to us."

And two years later, Jarvis writing in *Bloomberg*, said in an article entitled, "Dell Learns to Listen": "In the age of customers empowered by blogs and social media, Dell has leapt from worst to first."

Forbes tech reporter Shel Israel wrote, five years after its launch, "IdeaStorm has received nearly 15,000 suggestions and has made about 500 refinements based on them. Most were nice little tweaks such as backlit keyboards. . . . My favorite was ensuring that [Dell's] global support staff were fluent in the language that callers spoke." The article went on to describe how Dell hired one of Idea-Storm's most prolific idea contributors and most vocal critics to serve as the IdeaStorm community manager as it updated the platform in the interest of being even more responsive to the user community. IdeaStorm is still an active crowdsourcing forum for Dell and its customers. At the time of this writing, more than 35,000 ideas have been submitted on the site and more than 750,000 votes for those ideas have been cast by users.

The accolades that Dell received regarding its response to the "Dell Hell" customer hostility and the laptop battery recall were the fulfillment of a storyline we created in our fictional *Harvard Business Review* article. The vision casting exercise that informed our strategy became reality.

TAKEAWAYS

- ☐ **In a crisis, communicate** early and often.

- ☐ **Tell your stakeholders** what you know and what you don't know.

- ☐ **Fill the information vacuum.** If you don't, someone else will.

- ☐ **When you're working with insufficient information,** process can be your ally.

- ☐ **Use the digital and social media** platforms that your audience uses.

- ☐ **Communicate with a human voice** that captures the right tone for the moment.

- ☐ **Storytelling that appeals to emotion** can be a more powerful way to tell your narrative.

- ☐ **Imagine how you and your organization will be cast** in the story of the crisis—hero, villain, or victim?

- ☐ **Create the expectation** that something positive will come out of the crisis.

INTENSE SCRUTINY
FROM THE OUTSIDE

If you don't fill the information vacuum, someone else will do it for you.

4

A BURNING NEED TO
COMMUNICATE

"Crises and deadlocks, when they occur, have at least this advantage
—that they force us to think."
—*Jawaharlal Nehru, Prime Minister of India*

In August 2016, the South Korean electronics giant Samsung was
enthusiastic about prospects for its new Galaxy Note 7 smartphone.
Some consumer reviews had heralded it as the "best phone ever
made." Moreover, the company had brought the phone to market
weeks ahead of major competitor Apple and its new iPhone 7. That
optimism began to diminish when, for the first time, a Note 7 caught
fire in South Korea. However, Samsung pressed forward, introducing

the product in China after a prominent launch in the United States. Samsung was about to descend into a marketing nightmare.

Around the world, the Note 7 phones continued to overheat, catch fire, and explode.

By September, Samsung issued a recall for 2.5 million Note 7 phones, citing defective batteries. A few days later, the US Federal Aviation Administration advised airline passengers to avoid powering up the Samsung smart phones aboard aircraft or packing them in bags checked for the cargo hold. The next day, the US Consumer Product Safety Commission advised all Note 7 owners to stop using their phones. Three weeks later, a Southwest Airlines plane was evacuated because of a smoking Note 7 phone in the aircraft cabin.

Within a very short time, Samsung had a global communications crisis on its hands.

Not only was Samsung's reputation being tarnished by recalls and government advisories, but the brand was also being pummeled around the clock as consumers heard repeated warnings in the media, in airports, and aboard aircraft.

HOW DID SAMSUNG RESPOND?

Let's view the company's response through the lens of the five principles of crisis communication:

> Authenticity—The Samsung response suffered from the lack of a human face representing the company. And the initial communications were carefully worded in ways that did not acknowledge the severity of the problem and neglected

to include an apology. The early communications with consumers described an "exchange program" rather than the recall of a product that, as one critic described it in *The New York Times*, ". . . can literally catch fire and burn your house down with you in it." The response reflected a cold, institutional voice rather than a person or organization who cared.

Transparency—Early warnings of the fire risk were relegated to secondary pages on the Samsung website. To learn more about the threat consumers needed to click on a link labeled, "Updated Consumer Guidance for the Galaxy Note 7." That description hardly captured the urgency of the situation. And even this understated advisory did not immediately appear on Samsung's Facebook page or in its Twitter feed. Samsung's response seemed guarded and out of scale with the magnitude of the problem.

Transparency requires genuine conversations with your customers—listening to their concerns, anticipating and answering their questions. That was a challenge for an enormous, far-flung company like Samsung, especially given its Korean mindset and deference to authority. I lived in South Korea, and I saw how consumer relations often could be a one-way street, with a giant corporation only revealing information on its own terms and in accordance with its own timetable. By contrast, consumers in the West are only too happy to challenge authority and switch brand loyalty if they feel that they are being misled or information is being concealed. What started as a product problem at Samsung quickly morphed into a brand problem. Consumers could not be expected to buy and use Samsung's Note 7, or its other products, if they lost confidence in the company.

TRANSPARENCY REQUIRES GENUINE CONVERSATIONS WITH YOUR CUSTOMERS— LISTENING TO THEIR CONCERNS, ANTICIPATING AND ANSWERING THEIR QUESTIONS.

Speed—Samsung was painfully slow to respond to the crisis. Perhaps more importantly, an aggressive product launch schedule seems to have contributed to the debacle. Samsung built its reputation by introducing products that exemplified new technology and releasing them earlier than its rivals. Industry observers have stated that Samsung's delivery schedule, and its fixation on beating Apple to market, placed its engineers under deadline pressure that encouraged overly optimistic expectations and discounted safety concerns.

In addition, while speed is important, it cannot come at the expense of accuracy. Samsung made several assertions during the crisis that it was forced to retract. For instance, it assured customers in some markets that their phones used a different, safer battery than the ones with the incendiary defect. That turned out to be false. Then there was the replacement phone debacle, in which one million phones were returned and replaced with "safe" Note 7 smartphones. Amid all this, Samsung failed to comply with the protocols of the US Consumer Product Safety Commission in executing its recall. Then, less than two weeks later, the company halted all sales and production and told customers to stop using the Note 7 product.

While speed is important, it cannot come at the expense of accuracy.

As I have said elsewhere, process can be your friend. During a crisis, your stakeholders don't expect you to have all the answers, but you can earn trust and buy time by sharing what you are doing to manage the crisis while promising to provide more information as it becomes available. These questions could have been answered by Samsung in a timely and straightforward manner:

- What do you know about the cause of the problem?
- When did you learn about it?
- What are you doing to solve the problem?
- Do you care about the impact this is having on your customers, and what are you doing to make amends?
- When will you be able to share more information?

PROCESS CAN BE YOUR FRIEND.

But three months after the crisis, most of these questions remained unanswered. The Samsung website referred consumers to a microsite that addressed the recall and offered this apology, buried in a series of frequently asked questions about its exchange program: "We apologize for the inconvenience." Period.

If Samsung was listening to consumers, it chose to ignore many of their questions.

It was only on January 23, 2017—a year and four months after the problem with the Galaxy Note 7 first surfaced—that Samsung announced that it had determined that batteries made by two suppliers were the cause of the fires, as well as describing how a design flaw enabled the fires to occur.

> Agility—Samsung's delay in responding to the problem and the inaccuracy of its communications meant that it was constantly playing catch-up. The company's digital platforms were slow to disseminate critical information, and the whole operation lacked the agility to adapt to changing conditions. This was clearly aggravated by the rigid and inflexible culture at Samsung.

> Creativity—Samsung's internal culture is described by former employees as "top-down" and "militaristic." That kind of environment doesn't breed a great deal of creativity. There was nothing inventive or even resourceful about the content and dissemination of Samsung's consumer advisories.

It's no surprise that this crisis unfolded at a moment when Samsung was struggling with leadership succession and the retooling of its corporate culture. The founder and chairman of the company, Lee Kun-hee, was hospitalized in 2014 and remained so throughout the crisis. And while a transition of power to his son, Jay Y. Lee, was underway, that process was disrupted by charges of bribery against Jay Lee and his arrest by the South Korean government. These developments have added a shroud of mystery and uncertainty to a company already famous for its secrecy and lack of transparency. While Samsung is widely regarded as an electronics company in the West, in Korea it is a diversified behemoth that makes up nearly 20 percent of the nation's gross domestic product. South Koreans sometimes call their country the "Republic of Samsung," and the conglomerate's operations extend to ship building, chemicals, food products, appliances, theme parks, advertising, and life insurance. Nevertheless, Samsung's global brand largely rests on the performance of its electronics products.

The Samsung culture promotes swift development of new devices but does not empower rank-and-file employees to raise questions or take actions that might cause delays. "Samsung was a train wreck waiting to happen," a former employee told NPR. "They never expected any of their juniors to ever refuse any request asked of them. So it's basically an order. Anything that your supervisor or boss at Samsung says to you should be taken as a direct order from your commanding officer." Employees who question product safety could be regarded as troublemakers.

The source went on to describe how the company gave new employees a book of quotes by Chairman Lee and that employees joked about Lee Kun-hee being "Dear Leader," the title extended to the late Kim Jong-il, Supreme Leader of their neighbor to the north. "It seems a bit reminiscent of North Korea."

A GLOBAL PERSPECTIVE

NAVIGATING THE NUANCES OF CULTURE

Jin Montesano, Chief Public Affairs Office at Japan's LIXIL Group

Geo-cultural distinctions are essential to understanding and effectively managing a crisis, says Jin Montesano, chief public affairs officer at Japan's LIXIL Group and a veteran of public affairs and communications in Asia.

"Inserting your American perspective into multinational crises doesn't always help you win," says Montesano, a seasoned international crisis communications expert who has held senior positions at GE Capital, GlaxoSmithKline, and Kraft Foods. "Crises are local. They may have global implications. But you need to view the situation through the lens of the local stakeholders first. Multinational companies tend to think globally, and structures are in place to escalate crises quickly to HQ. If you are overly focused on the shareholders' interests, rather than local interests, it may distort your ability to make the right decisions. It may make you take a tougher stance that could undermine your brand. I don't think investors' interests should be the immediate focus in the midst of a crisis."

She cautions that local executives may be overly deferential to crisis specialists from corporate headquarters. Rather than assertively offering advice about the local situation, "the local team may let the international bigwigs and crisis team from HQ take over. In doing so, the local voice and expertise may get lost in the early moments of decision-making as the business navigates the crisis." Montesano says now more than ever, multinational companies need solid communications expertise at the management table when operating in risky foreign markets. "Companies need to invest in strategic communications professionals who can hold their own with the other members of the management team. Companies tend to want to bunker down during a crisis, but good communicators bring the local stakeholder's interests into the board room when decisions are being made."

Cultural knowledge is crucial to effective communications. For example, Montesano points out that in Japan the public places more trust in search engine results than in media generated by human editors, according to data from the 2017 Edelman Trust Barometer.

Cultural knowledge is crucial to effective communications.

"And in countries like Japan, you must apologize," she says. "For many American companies, there's the inclination to never admit fault. But in Japan, apologizing has nothing to do with legal liability. It's about business etiquette; it's about recognizing your responsibility in a situation and asking for the patience of the people who have been inconvenienced by your company's actions. In a crisis, apologizing is essential to opening up a dialogue with the public and the media."

Estimates of the loss in market value experienced by Samsung have ranged from $5 billion to $20 billion.

Samsung apologized for the Note 7 debacle in full-page newspaper ads in *The Wall Street Journal*, *The New York Times*, and *The Washington Post* in the first week of November 2016, two months after the first recall of the phones.

Considering the remarkable, intense scrutiny that every Samsung action received, it is worth reviewing some of the key strategies that other organizations have used in crisis.

I have talked about the importance of a digital command center. One of our clients, a global airline, developed a cross-functional command center that included a control room, conference room, and social media pods that cover online and social media conversations 24 hours a day, seven days a week. We helped establish the center, which functions as the intelligence gathering arm of the organization. The first major benefit was that the airline started listening to its customers in a more comprehensive and sophisticated way. The center, a large room that now houses dozens of digital and social media specialists, includes large screens that chart trends in digital and social media conversations about the brand. The center enables the company to learn not just how customers feel about issues the airline regards as important, but to understand what customers and the public care about.

The fact that it is cross-functional also provides a benefit. Corporate communications, marketing, and customer service all shared space in the original command center. That kept social media from being relegated to a corporate communications responsibility or a marketing responsibility and helped integrate it as a priority for the whole organization. Samsung's social media channels were more focused on posting promotional content rather than trustworthy information about the crisis.

We also helped the airline develop online conversation analysis to provide an overall sense of general sentiment about the brand, as well as specific issues that were creating commentary. When you have sophisticated analysis of the conversation, then you can make more informed, data-driven decisions about how to respond to problems.

Online monitoring also gives you a sense of the public argument—why do people feel a certain way about your brand? It increases your ability to understand the views of people on both sides of an argument, giving you greater empathy. It also helps you understand perceptions that are based on misinformation, which happens frequently in social media, and to create strategies to correct the record and shape the public discussion. If the company isn't responding to an issue or a line of criticism, it creates a vacuum that can be filled with misinformation, alarmist views, and conspiracy theories.

"Why did the company change its policy that way?" some might ask on social media. "It must be prejudiced. That's appalling!" We do live in the age of outrage, and social media can take outlandish leaps

When you have sophisticated analysis of the conversation, then you can make more informed, data-driven decisions about how to respond to problems.

ACCURATE INFORMATION CAN FILL THE VACUUM AND QUIET THE OUTRAGE.

of logic and transform them into tantalizing click bait, especially for people who are already critical of your brand. Accurate information can fill the vacuum and quiet the outrage.

The airline took social media a step farther by establishing a dedicated customer service process within social media. If a customer complains or comments about a travel problem on social media, the company will process the complaint exactly as if the customer had dialed its call center. The philosophy is that the company will resolve issues in the customer's preferred medium. That could be Twitter, email, phone, or via the website. However, it's important that if you make this commitment, you do it to scale. The goal is consistency, so you must commit to each platform and staff it accordingly.

DETERMINING THE SCALE OF A RESPONSE

Our team at ICF has developed escalation protocols for numerous clients to help with decision-making in a crisis. The point is to avoid overreacting. There are many situations where releasing a follow-up statement about an issue creates a second news cycle for the story. You can end up exposing more people to a negative perception without winning the hearts and minds of your critics. Sometimes a rumor or piece of misinformation supports a partisan customer's core beliefs in a way that they cannot be dissuaded under any circumstances.

The benefit of a protocol is that it provides a framework, in advance, for how, when, and to what extent you should respond to a problem. The protocol is based on evidence and experience. As such, it can have a rational, calming effect on jangled nerves, and decisions may then be guided by data rather than emotions.

Escalation protocols should be based on these guiding principles:

- Avoid fanning the flames—Social media by nature empowers communities of like-minded critics. If you respond to every small, niche issue in social media, you may end up giving your critics a much wider audience.

- Tell your own story—If an issue is likely to gain momentum, you want your customers and the public to hear it from you first. Being first allows you to frame the narrative and get the facts straight. An escalation protocol provides evidence-based insight into whether an issue will expand to a larger audience.

- Choose accuracy over speed—Speed is important, especially in social media. But releasing inaccurate information can be more damaging, and costly, than a slow response. The goal is accuracy *and* speed.

We frequently design issues management protocols that include three levels of escalation—A, B, and C. An A-Level threshold means a serious issue with a wide audience that could become a crisis. A crisis response could be triggered by reaching specified thresholds in:

- Online volume (posts or citations);
- Mainstream media articles about the issue;
- Digital influencer articles about the issue;
- Posts on the company's social media channels;
- Major advocacy groups raising the issue.

Lower levels of activity would trigger a Level B or Level C response, which would involve smaller, more targeted actions to address the issue being raised online and in social media.

In the meantime, standby messages are crafted for all predictable problems to be ready in the event of a crisis. Weather, terrorism, food safety, employee malfeasance, website crashes, equipment failures, and data breaches are examples of predictable challenges for which statements are prepared in advance.

In addition to standby messages, thorough crisis preparedness requires the creation of a "dark website" to serve as an information hub. This site would be activated in the event of a very serious event, giving the company a website solely devoted to addressing the crisis in ways that are more robust than the typical company site. This allows the company's home page to continue to focus on ongoing operations while the information needs of the crisis are better served on the single-purpose site.

Throughout much of the Samsung fiasco, its homepage appeared unconcerned about the hazardous phones because the site was trying to do too many things at once.

In addition, some companies may also need a full-time website that's used exclusively for news. It can serve as a hub for credible, trustworthy news about the company—in good times and bad. Content can be shared in social media with links back to the news site. However, if you take this route, you must cultivate meaningful traffic to the news site to be effective. This usually means having a budget for paid promotion and sponsored content. Without adequate traffic, the dedicated news site is just window dressing.

Once there is a crisis, your brand is especially vulnerable if a similar incident recurs. Critics and customers will point to the previous event and surmise that the new episode indicates a pattern of neglect or incompetence. Companies that experience crises need to be especially vigilant to avoid a similar failure. You must double down on your efforts to prevent a recurrence.

CRISIS CAN MAGNIFY THE NEED FOR CHANGE

One of the greatest challenges for leaders is to recognize when a crisis is caused by a need for change. The natural tendency is to defend your business model and to resist attack from the outside—to focus on why your business practices and culture are right and your critics are wrong. But crisis can be a time to hit the pause button and reconsider your actions in the context of societal change.

The Tylenol crisis led to a revolution in product packaging. Tylenol introduced the triple-sealed consumer product that became an industry standard. The 2016 crisis at the Cincinnati Zoo, where a 3-year-old child entered a gorilla enclosure and a 440-pound gorilla was shot and killed, forced us to reexamine the keeping of large primates in captivity. Indeed, within days of the crisis, an article appeared in *The New York Times* entitled, "Do Gorillas Even Belong in Zoos? Harambe's Death Spurs Debate."

Winston Churchill is credited with the expression, "Never let a good crisis go to waste." Because crisis brings added visibility and risk, a company will be highly motivated to invest in a solution. The purse strings are not held so tightly in a crisis. It's a way to accelerate progress and problem-solving. For a brief period following crisis, the entire company may be committed to rebuilding its reputation and earning back the trust of stakeholders.

After adjusting its corporate strategy and culture, Samsung may emerge from the crisis a stronger company. It may be better equipped to manage public expectations, changing values, and an environment where management not only talks, but listens. Indeed, Samsung reported that profits for the final quarter of 2016 were up 50 percent, reaching its highest level in three years, despite the Galaxy Note 7 debacle.

TAKEAWAYS

☐ **When experiencing intense scrutiny from the outside,** make sure your response demonstrates authenticity, transparency, speed, agility, and creativity.

☐ **A digital command center** can give you invaluable insights into your customers' concerns, misinformation swirling in the marketplace, and reputational problems—before they reach a crisis level.

☐ **Avoid fanning the flames.** An escalation protocol can help keep you from overreacting.

☐ **If there's bad news,** make sure your customers hear it from you first.

☐ **Choose accuracy** over speed.

☐ **Consider building a "dark site"** to have at the ready for crisis management.

☐ **Crisis offers opportunity,** but you must seize it.

ESCALATING
FLOW OF EVENTS

Things will probably get worse before they get better.

5

MELTDOWN AT FUKUSHIMA

"Mankind has never faced the forces of physics and the forces of nature that were confronted at Fukushima."
—Charles Casto, Former Regional Administrator,
US Nuclear Regulatory Commission

On March 11, 2011, a magnitude 9.0 earthquake struck off the northeast coast of Japan's main island of Honshu. It was the most powerful quake ever recorded in that country. The Tokyo Electric Power Company (TEPCO) owned and operated two nuclear power plants in the immediate region, known as Tohoku, with a total of 10 nuclear reactors. (A third TEPCO nuclear plant, the world's largest, is at Kashiwazaki-Kariwa in Niigata Prefecture on the opposite side of the island, outside the earthquake zone.) In a testament to Japanese skills at seismic safety, all the nuclear facilities in the Fukushima region survived the massive earthquake intact and automatically shut down exactly as they were designed to do.

What has become known as the Great East Japan Earthquake knocked out external power to TEPCO's six-reactor Daiichi plant. Electric power is essential to powering the cooling systems that keep the fuel assemblies within the reactors from overheating, melting down, destroying the facility, and causing a public safety and environmental calamity. It is also essential to cooling the water in the pools in which spent fuel is stored and which, though no longer potent enough to power the reactors, still must be shielded by water to avoid radiation from escaping into the atmosphere.

Diesel-powered backup generators are designed to switch on during a power failure to provide the necessary electricity until the electrical grid is restored. And that's what happened at the Daiichi plant—until the next crisis arrived. (The Daini plant, only a few miles down the coast, was less affected by the tsunami and retained just enough external power to avoid disaster.)

The massive earthquake, which roiled the Tohoku region for an agonizing six minutes, also propelled enormous tsunami waves as high as 52 feet. The seawall protecting the plant, only 30 feet above sea level, was not designed to withstand such a crushing wall of water. Seven giant waves, approximately two and a half times higher than the plant was built to withstand, crashed over the seawall and into the facility. Two employees drowned when the waves struck the plant. The tsunami smashed buildings, hurled ships inland, swept

MAP OF NORTHEAST JAPAN

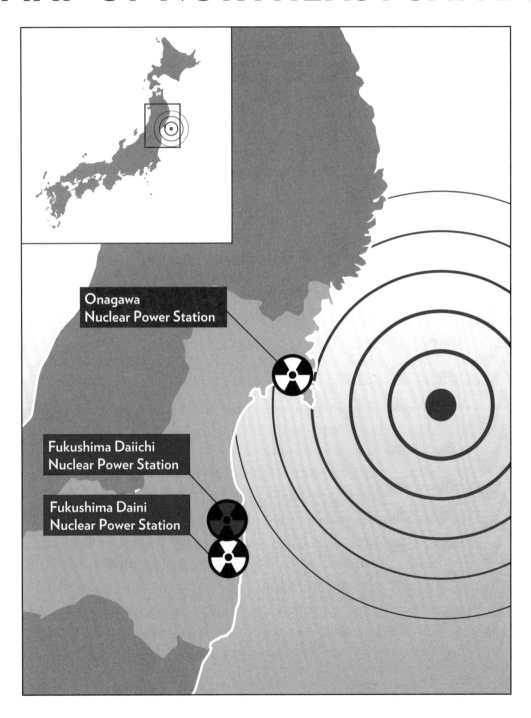

Onagawa
Nuclear Power Station

Fukushima Daiichi
Nuclear Power Station

Fukushima Daini
Nuclear Power Station

away airplanes at the airport, and inundated large areas of northeastern Japan. Some 18,500 lives would be lost to the tsunami.

Then an even bigger threat became apparent. About an hour after the earthquake, the backup diesel generators shut down. People in TEPCO's control center at Daiichi had only sketchy knowledge of the scale of the damage from the tsunami. Employees with flashlights were sent to the turbine buildings to check on the generators. They reported that the basements where the generators were located were full of water. In the darkened control center, supervisors could not believe that seawater had entered the buildings—it was inconceivable that the basements could be flooded. But it was true. The plant had lost its emergency power source. In industry parlance, it was an SBO—Station Black Out.

"*Yabai!*" someone screamed. "We're in trouble!"

What followed was a race against time during which one piece of bad news was rapidly followed by another. "Mankind has never faced the forces of physics and the forces of nature that were confronted at Fukushima," said Charles Casto, former Regional Administrator at the United States Nuclear Regulatory Commission, who would later become director of site operations for the NRC in Fukushima.

Of the six reactors at Fukushima Daiichi, only Units 1, 2, and 3 were operating when the tsunami struck and cooling systems failed. Crews risked their lives to relieve pressure in the reactors by venting them to the outside, which prevented an even larger catastrophe, but they could not prevent the fuel cores in the three reactors from melting down. In addition, the radioactive uranium inside the fuel rods combined with other elements in the reactor core to create hydrogen gas, which began to collect beneath the roof of the buildings. It was only a matter of time before something would ignite the hydrogen. The next day, an explosion blew the roof off the Unit 1 reactor building. Eventually, two more explosions would follow, one of them from Unit 4 which, although spared from meltdown because it wasn't operating, suffered an explosion when a shared exhaust stack with Unit 3 provided a route for hydrogen to accumulate inside the building.

The Fukushima disaster was the product of unprecedented natural phenomena, siting and design imperfections of the era, technological constraints, and just plain bad luck. The failures that would emerge from the events of March 2011, and many more that would come in the months to follow, have caused the nuclear power industry to reconsider many of its safety assumptions and, in the long run, to become even safer. But it also is a textbook lesson in the immense global consequences of imperfect communications.

The focus of this chapter is the fourth stage of crisis—escalating flow of events. In a crisis, you should assume:

- You don't know everything, but lack of information does not justify paralysis.

- Things are probably worse than you think.

- You need to communicate what you do know, when you know it.

- More events are coming.

Fukushima surely stands as one of the most pronounced examples of an escalating flow of events. There were many unknowable facts. The situation was worse than anyone anticipated. And more crisis was on its way.

In fact, the recovery process, now more than six years under way, has brought a series of crises as TEPCO, Japan's government, and the international nuclear community have struggled to determine effective strategies for cleaning up the Daiichi site and decommissioning the damaged reactors. Almost immediately, focus on the ultimate goal—removing the molten fuel debris and other contaminants—became obscured by the challenges of managing water.

Standing between the mountain and the sea, the Daiichi facility had massive amounts of naturally occurring groundwater flowing into the cracked foundations of the reactor buildings, mixing with contaminated cooling water, and flowing into the ocean. The intense publicity and environmental fears associated with the water management challenge at Fukushima were so intense that TEPCO's ability, or inability, to manage the water problem became for many the barometer by which its overall ability to manage the disaster would be judged. *The New York Times*, for example, called for the Japanese government to take over the cleanup because of the overwhelming scale of the water management problem.

The communications challenges at TEPCO required that it respond to a series of ongoing crises while simultaneously attempting to rebuild confidence in the company's operations and its tarnished reputation. TEPCO, which for decades had been a local utility with little if any reason to communicate outside Japan, especially on a matter of such magnitude in a crisis environment, was clearly in over its head. Inside Japan, the company was under attack for sluggish and incomplete disclosures; outside, the criticism was equally harsh, with the added challenges of a significant language barrier.

Asked what he learned from the events of 2011 and its resulting challenges, Naomi Hirose, president of TEPCO, said: "After the accident, I should have seen things from the position and emotional perspective of the local residents, not just what was happening on the site itself."

MANAGING CRISIS, REBUILDING TRUST

My team and I were brought into the situation more than a year after the acute phase of the crisis. We were referred to TEPCO by Dr. Dale Klein, former chairman of the US Nuclear Regulatory Commission. He is a distinguished professor of engineering at The University of Texas at Austin, where I serve as adjunct professor in the Moody College of Communication. Soon after the accident, Klein was named chair of the independent Nuclear Reform Monitoring Committee appointed by TEPCO to advise on safety culture, emergency preparedness, risk management, and risk communication. Klein immediately recognized that the Fukushima events involved both failures of emergency preparedness and communication. He asked me and my team at ICF to bring TEPCO communications into the 21st century, not by merely correcting problems, but by building competencies within the company. "I want you to teach them to how to fish and not merely catch the fish for them," Klein instructed. In other words, he wanted us to help develop the TEPCO team, so they could manage the issues for the long haul.

In the aftermath of the Fukushima disaster, there was a tremendous public mistrust of TEPCO, both in Japan and in the international nuclear energy and safety community. Some of the mistrust was the result of poor decision-making, a culture of non-disclosure, and flawed communications strategy. But the public skepticism and lack of confidence was also caused by factors as simple as publishing poor English translations of documents, weak messaging, a lack of timeliness, and poor visual communication. We determined that it was imperative that we regain the confidence of the international community, the global nuclear industry, and key influencers.

Klein recognized that Japanese culture has a more hierarchal chain of command than in the West, and that such an attitude discouraged rank-and-file employees from raising safety issues. "When the boss tells you something, you do it," said Klein. "We needed to change their culture, and we needed to change their communication." TEPCO's leadership understood that change was essential and has helped promote the concept that it's okay to challenge authority in the interest of safety.

We also recognized that we needed to restore confidence with two key constituencies in Japan: women, who have greater skepticism of nuclear energy, and fishermen, whose livelihoods depend on healthy water quality and who had been kept from fishing in waters near Fukushima since the accident.

Lady Barbara Judge, an American-British lawyer and businesswoman who serves as deputy chair of the TEPCO Nuclear Reform

"AFTER THE ACCIDENT, I SHOULD HAVE SEEN THINGS FROM THE POSITION AND EMOTIONAL PERSPECTIVE OF THE LOCAL RESIDENTS, NOT JUST WHAT WAS HAPPENING ON THE SITE ITSELF."

—NAOMI HIROSE, PRESIDENT OF TEPCO

Monitoring Committee, made it part of her mission to reach out to women. "It is often said that in every country, not just Japan, one of the groups in society that is the most against nuclear energy is women, particularly upper-middle class women. Accordingly, I think it is important to have someone who can view and assess a safety culture from the point of view of a woman, as well as a nuclear expert."

When viewed from the perspective of the five principles of crisis communications, TEPCO clearly needed help in all areas:

> Authenticity—Inferior communications and the opaque corporate culture at TEPCO portrayed the company as lacking openness and candor.
>
> Transparency—As a local utility that acted as a near-monopoly, the company did not have a history of robust engagement with customers and the media. Communications had not been a priority and the communications function itself was typically not staffed with career communications professionals.
>
> Speed—A weak communications team with low status in the organization and without an active voice in the executive suite, combined with inadequate English language translation skills and poorly developed digital platforms, left the company slow and unresponsive.
>
> Agility—The company was not accustomed to listening to the digital conversation, so it was difficult for it to recognize stakeholder issues and respond to them. The

escalating flow of events was so overwhelming that it would have challenged any organization, but the lack of career communications professionals at TEPCO, and the strategic thinking they would bring to the situation, was problematic.

Creativity—TEPCO didn't have the means to create compelling content or to tell its story effectively through digital channels. It was dependent on dense, poorly illustrated, and badly constructed press releases largely written by engineers. Video and other visual content, when created at all, was more appropriate to a technical engineering conference than a general audience.

In addition, TEPCO's website was relatively primitive and difficult to navigate, leaving the company bereft of digital tools to convey important messages when the company urgently needed to communicate with stakeholders.

My team and I assessed the situation and recommended that TEPCO pursue several communications objectives.

Structural Change—TEPCO needed to strengthen its organization, communications skills, and strategic thinking. This meant less reactive and tactical communication and more emphasis on communicating strategically and proactively. Primarily, that meant thinking carefully about the intended net impact of communications—rather than simply responding to inquiries—and crafting key messages intended to produce that impact. It also required humanizing the company by moving away from communications based on engineering reports and impersonal corporate language. We also recommended hiring several communications professionals who could focus on English-language and international audiences. Building internal capacity for precise English translations that would permit timely communications was a high priority. Overall, the company needed to elevate the role of communications and restructure its organization charts accordingly.

We provided extensive media and crisis preparedness training for TEPCO executives and to the communications staff, both in Japan and in the United States. We also developed an issue escalation protocol to help TEPCO determine when an issue becomes significant enough to warrant a response—or if issuing a statement would just give the story more weight, leading to greater media coverage.

The guiding principles in issue escalation:

- Own our story, even if it's negative. We don't want to let media or other actors twist or subvert an issue. Sharing our story and providing the TEPCO perspective first is often the best way to effectively manage the issue.

- Don't fan the flames. Without mainstream media attention, many issues subside and do not require a response. Our decision calculus must consider whether a communications response will do more harm than good.

The escalation protocol helps predict if the issue will gain significant traction in the absence of a TEPCO response. Once our monitoring systems identify an issue, then we assess the impact. Among the questions we consider:

- Is there a health/safety concern?
- Is the company being perceived as uncaring or unresponsive?
- Is the company being accused of violating its core values?
- Is there significant commentary online or in the media?
- Is this an issue that will interest the international community?

Next we look at response triggers, such as the volume of articles/website visitors/posts in social media, and determine whether advocacy groups (environmental, protestor, evacuee, customer) are involved. We have established three thresholds based on objective criteria that inform the scale of TEPCO's response. The protocol also helps determine the optimal medium in which to respond as well as the tone, context, and supporting information required. Having this matrix prepared in advance helps speed decision-making during a crisis and helps avoid mistakes in the heat of the moment.

We've seen reputation-threatening issues gather momentum online, and responding appropriately is critical to protecting TEPCO's reputation. Because of our listening and escalation protocols, we have access to more data with which to make informed decisions. By creating a predictable process that calculates the severity, volume, sentiment, influencer engagement, and mainstream media coverage, the decision-making can be more rapid and more evidence-based.

Content Quality—Prior to the Great East Japan Earthquake, TEPCO had not needed to engage in sophisticated international communications. For the most part, it had communicated with shareholders, customers, and government agencies—in Japanese. All that changed after the Fukushima crisis. TEPCO's vulnerability to the earthquake and tsunami and the challenges posed by the recovery had major implications for the nuclear power industry and governments across the globe. It was imperative that TEPCO communicate accurately and effectively, taking advantage of all the available digital tools and strategies. We set about helping the company develop the capacity to produce engaging and informative photography, infographics, videos, and graphic design. We also helped the company make strategic hires of specialists in digital communications and information visualization. In a world where "content is king," TEPCO needed to tell its story and convey important information in compelling ways.

By creating a predictable process that calculates the severity, volume, sentiment, influencer engagement, and mainstream media coverage, the decision-making can be more rapid and more evidence-based.

As an example of telling the TEPCO story through visualization, our team developed an infographic to inform stakeholders about new safety measures, based on lessons learned from Fukushima, at one of the company's other nuclear facilities. It was entitled "8 Ways Kashiwazaki-Kariwa Aims to Become the World's Safest Nuclear Power Plant." In eight simple panels, the infographic illustrates important information about improvements to flood prevention, backup reactor cooling systems, and terrorism safety.

Expanding Digital Assets—TEPCO's website was not up to international standards, and its presence in social media was ineffective. The website was redesigned to be responsive to mobile devices, to integrate more easily with video and social media, and to include more interactive content. Twitter and Facebook activity was increased, with greater emphasis on photos, video, and graphics and on linking content to TEPCO's website.

Listening and Measurement—My team and I established an online listening command center that provides a real-time, data-driven basis for communications decisions. The listening operations permit TEPCO to track key conversations about the Fukushima disaster, the clean up, and nuclear power safety on a daily and weekly basis. Monitoring efforts also function as an early warning system for breaking news and potential crises. It was also necessary to closely link Japanese-language digital conversations to the international communications team. Conversations that begin in Japanese digital media often migrate to international English-language media as they are picked up by the Tokyo-based Japanese-speaking correspondents for Western media.

We developed a Weekly Listening and Performance Management Dashboard to provide clear analytics on digital communications and outcomes. The dashboard recorded metrics on digital communications volume (total and by platform), topic categories, influencer volume, trending articles, message penetration, and engagement volume. It also showed examples of the week's top performing content.

But creating metrics for one company in isolation doesn't provide enough context to get the most insight into performance. Going a step further, we created a Social Media Performance Index that quantified and assigned weighted values for audience size, average engagement per post, quality of content, and community management. These metrics were applied to Twitter, Facebook, and YouTube. We then applied the criteria to two American utility companies and one Japanese utility that represented best-in-class competitors from our point of view. That gave TEPCO a direct benchmark comparison within its industry for multiple criteria, as well as a baseline from which to measure progress.

Some of the criteria used in the analysis:

> Content—Interactivity (clicks, tags, interactions with influencers), relevance (to targeted markets, such as international audiences), syndication (publishing content from other sources), and visual appeal (stimulating links, imagery, strong design). A high score would reflect content that contains uniformly compelling language, tone, visuals,

and links tailored to targeted audiences. The content features embedded videos, eye-catching photos, easily comprehensible language, and strong hooks with links.

Interaction—Content is highly interactive, with links, videos, and calls to action. Posts tag or mention fans and influencers and encourage conversation. (Influencers are defined as major media outlets, nuclear industry advocates and detractors, as well as key political figures that drive conversation on TEPCO-related issues.) Polls, videos, games, and other brand-related content encourage conversation.

Community Management—Assigned values for consistency (in language, tone, and voice), organization and frequency (cohesive content, systematic tagging, and responsiveness). High values for frequent audience interaction through asking questions, participating in conversations, and submission of audience photos and videos. Community managers respond to questions in a timely manner and with a distinct personality.

The dashboards and Social Media Performance Index helped demonstrate that there are utility companies, despite their often being characterized as sleepy and less engaging than consumer product companies, that are doing exemplary work in digital communications. My team and I observed that when provided with empirical data, the benchmark studies, and examples of best practices within its industry, TEPCO became more receptive to change and more convinced of the value of digital communications. It was a powerful example of showing rather than telling to help the client adopt a new strategy.

Trust and Credibility—We needed to increase trust in TEPCO. A constellation of factors combined to severely erode the company's reputation for accuracy and reliable information. The ability of the company to recover from the crisis, to effectively remediate the public health, property, and environmental damages, and to share what it learned from the experience depended on the public and the world at large believing what TEPCO was saying.

We placed a high priority on transparency, authenticity, and on humanizing communications. We relied heavily on CEO Naomi Hirose and Chief Decommissioning Officer Naohiro Masuda to serve as the faces of TEPCO. Hirose, Yale-educated and a fluent English speaker, became CEO after the accident and is highly regarded in Japan and internationally. Masuda, who as superintendent at Fukushima Daiini was the leader of its successful effort to prevent an accident similar to the one that destroyed Daiichi, had been put in charge of the Daiichi cleanup.

The unprecedented scale and complexity of the Fukushima cleanup has offered an opportunity. TEPCO and its leadership are becoming authorities in developing safety practices, cleanup technologies, and environmental protocols, and have committed themselves to sharing that knowledge with the world. We have helped TEPCO reach out to third-party experts and organizations to help share the knowledge acquired from the crisis. The worldwide nuclear industry, which itself had been hurt by the generally negative global reaction to nuclear power after the Fukushima accident, was happy to participate. TEPCO received tremendous cooperation from the international nuclear industry as the company tried to rebuild trust.

LESSONS FROM FUKUSHIMA

For example, my team worked with the Howard Baker Forum on Energy to produce a video series, "Lessons from Fukushima." The Forum, named for the late US senator and ambassador to Japan Howard Baker, is devoted to public policy and international affairs. The video series was published by the Forum on its website and posted on its social media platforms.

One statement from the series, by former Nuclear Regulatory Commission senior official Charles Casto, who served as director of site operations for the NRC in Fukushima, spoke to the legacy of Fukushima:

> The industry has to have the belief that these accidents can happen or they'll never prepare for them. . . . The other legacy was how well TEPCO responded in the end, how well TEPCO coordinated with the rest of the world . . . The decommissioning work at Fukushima Daiichi has advanced decommissioning technology greatly. Every day at Fukushima Daiichi they are developing new tools, new technologies, and new strategies to decommission nuclear plants far beyond the strategies and the

FUKUSHIMA 50

technologies that we had prior to Fukushima. This advancement will carry the industry forward with new robotics, instrumentation, and strategies.

The video series benefited TEPCO by showcasing the expert opinions of influencers who have both the credibility and the digital channels to tell the story of the cleanup objectively.

Another example was in 2016 when my team at ICF planned an industry briefing to mark the fifth anniversary of Fukushima. The event was co-sponsored by the Nuclear Energy Institute (NEI) and held at the National Press Club in Washington, DC. The NEI announced that during the five years since Fukushima, US nuclear energy facilities had invested more than $4 billion and devoted thousands of person-hours to better ensure safety in the face of extreme events such as Fukushima. The chief operating officer of NEI chaired the event, which was attended by top nuclear industry officials, regulators, and the media. The briefing included presentations from the chief nuclear officer at TEPCO, former NRC chairman Dale Klein, and Miles O'Brien, an influential science journalist. As a result, TEPCO was positioned in the role of being at the vanguard of the latest safety developments in nuclear power while helping to advance Japan's carbon emissions goals by ensuring that nuclear power fulfills its role in Japan's national energy policy.

Mainstream media covering the event included *Time*, *The Huffington Post*, *Bloomberg*, *BBC News*, and *The Japan Times*. The briefing received more than 30,000 online mentions and cast TEPCO as being an important part of the solution to future challenges in harnessing nuclear energy. It also reinforced key TEPCO executives as thought leaders and subject-matter experts.

The phenomenon of the "Fukushima 50," mentioned briefly in an earlier chapter, has helped reorient some of the public antipathy toward TEPCO. The moniker refers to the original 50 employees who stayed at Daiichi after approximately 750 employees were evacuated. Actually, the initial 50 would be later joined by scores of engineers, technicians, firefighters, and rank-and-file workers from multiple organizations who struggled to stabilize the plant's reactors while placing themselves at great personal risk. They fought flooding, fires, explosions, and radiation poisoning. Only the enormous efforts and sacrifices made by these workers spared further destruction and greater environmental calamity. Various media have praised the bravery and selflessness of the "Fukushima 50," and they have been honored in the international press and even in the lyrics of popular music.

OPENING THE DOOR OF TRANSPARENCY

Another way to promote trust, confidence, and transparency is to open your doors to influential storytellers to allow objective reporting. We advised TEPCO to accept an unprecedented offer from the PBS science series *NOVA*. The goal was to convey a balanced and informed view of TEPCO's progress at Fukushima and its other nuclear facilities. We believed this would help build trust in the company and its cleanup operations.

In preparation, we developed a communications plan for the

ANOTHER WAY TO PROMOTE TRUST, CONFIDENCE, AND TRANSPARENCY IS TO OPEN YOUR DOORS TO INFLUENTIAL STORYTELLERS TO ALLOW OBJECTIVE REPORTING.

premier of the *NOVA* documentary that included developing supporting materials, developing content to syndicate on digital platforms with appropriate tags and hashtags, and deploying our digital listening command center to follow the online conversation. We also increased reach on digital platforms by sharing the link to the PBS/ *NOVA* documentary video with news outlets, influencers, and key stakeholders.

The resulting one-hour documentary told the story of the Fukushima crisis in great detail and with a tone sympathetic to the enormous challenges faced by TEPCO leadership and its workers.

Partly as the result of a robot failure at TEPCO's Daiichi plant, we became aware of a high level of media interest in the use of robotics in the nuclear power industry. TEPCO asked us to prepare a strategy for reaching digital influencers in the field of robotics for the purpose of engaging them in future stories, albeit with more successful narratives. My team created two tiers of key digital influencers made up of business thought leaders such as Bill Gates, authoritative agencies such as the US Department of Energy, the Defense Advanced Research Projects Agency (DARPA), environmental experts, energy insiders, and influential journalists with strong interests in robotics. We created an index that measured reach (size of audience), resonance (measurable impact based on audience engagement), and relevance (influencer's affinity for TEPCO key messages). In the months and years ahead, TEPCO can use this digital influencer outreach plan to help design messages and communications that more effectively tell the story of the role of robotics at Fukushima.

TEPCO's Nuclear Monitoring Reform Committee requested periodic updates on TEPCO's communications initiatives. Our team at ICF prepared thorough reviews in 2014 and 2016. The 2014 review covered crisis preparedness, web content, strategic messaging, and online listening and monitoring. The main topics of the 2016 review were organization and skills, content quality, social media performance, and trust. The preparation of the reports included interviews with senior executives of the company, members of the communications team, members of the media who regularly cover TEPCO, representatives of key foreign embassies in Tokyo, and key international influencers and staff members of the Nuclear Energy Institute. These communications assessments have helped TEPCO establish strategic communications goals and pursue them in a systematic way, using sophisticated digital metrics to measure performance.

One of the things we always want to explore is the opportunity to tell our story in the context of a current event or significant date that provides relevance or context. The fifth anniversary of Fukushima was an obvious example—the chance to mark the date of the tragedy and to report progress. It served to transform expertise acquired in the aftermath of crisis into international thought leadership. The initial experiments with robots in the cleanup were not entirely successful, but they helped us to think about robotics as a way to tell our story effectively in the future.

Finally, we are advising TEPCO on preparations for the 2020 Olympic Games. The Olympics will bring many advocacy groups to Japan to leverage the international visibility of the Games. Some of those groups will oppose nuclear power. But there will also be

TIER 1 DIGITAL INFLUENCERS

THE CELEBRITY	THE AUTHORITY	THE ANALYST	
An entertainment or business person with notoriety.	A trusted source of information, typically an organization.	A researcher seeking and providing credible insights.	
SAMANTHA WATSON	**ANDREW PHILLIPS**	**HENRY BROOKESTONE**	
Prominent actress and activist who frequently tweets on environmental threats and policy. She has been a keynote speaker at multiple symposia on environmental protection and Earth Day events. **Santa Monica, CA**	Chair of the Environmental Defense Trust, former deputy administrator of the EPA, and current partner in the Washington law firm of Scott, Phillips & Thompson. Adjunct professor at Columbia. **New York, NY**	Chair of the Department of Environmental Sciences at the University of North Carolina and principal investigator of a major grant from the EPA. Author of the most-cited textbook on the influence of air quality on health. **Chapel Hill, NC**	
 Reach Resonance Relevance	 Reach Resonance Relevance	 Reach Resonance Relevance	
TOTAL INFLUENCER SCORE			
43.7	5.3	48.2	

Reach

Reach is the general audience size (or followers) an influencer has on social platforms.

Resonance

Resonance is the measurable impact of an influencer's posted content, typically derived from audience engagement.

The following profiles describe a hypothetical situation and represent examples of individual influencers and categories. Tier 1 represents those influencers who are ideal content partners due to their audience reach and impact, as well as their relevance to the industry. However, given their high profiles, Tier 1 influencers may be difficult to reach.

THE EXPERT	THE INSIDER	THE JOURNALIST
An individual known for thought leadership in a given field(s).	An individual with access to industry policy makers.	An individual reporting on related industry news.
CHARLIE LANCING	**JAMES RYDELL**	**CATHERINE MCKENZIE**
Former chief scientist for Gulf Chemicals with moderate views on environmental issues. Respected by industry and members of the environmental movement. Board member of the Sierra Club. **Houston, TX**	Former executive director of the American Chemical Institute, prominent Washington lobbyist. Takes the lead on environmentally sensitive legislation affecting the chemical and refining industries. **Washington, D.C.**	Independent reporter and producer of news and documentaries covering science and the environment. Host of a PBS series on health and the environment that won Scripps Howard and Peabody Awards. Frequently appears on CNN for commentary regarding environmental accidents. **Boston, MA**
Reach Resonance Relevance	Reach Resonance Relevance	Reach Resonance Relevance
18.6	**42.5**	**36.2**

Relevance
Relevance describes whether an influencer's posted content aligns with the company's key messages and priority topics.

opportunities to share the positive developments that have emerged from Fukushima. The 2016 Rio de Janeiro Olympics demonstrated how the event can cast light on the environment, crime, water quality, security, and international activism, as well as how the international media can magnify all these storylines while covering the Games.

We will continue to help TEPCO tell the story of how its experiences in the aftermath of the Great East Japan Earthquake have advanced the nuclear power industry and enhanced related safety standards around the world.

TAKEAWAYS

- [ ] **In cascading crisis,** things will probably get worse before they get better.

- [ ] **To be effective,** the communications team must have a seat in the executive suite.

- [ ] **Communicate what you know,** when you know it.

- [ ] **A lack of transparency and authenticity in crisis** can damage your reputation for years to come.

- [ ] **In international crisis management,** precise translations are essential to your communications.

- [ ] **Even quiet companies that keep a low profile** need a professional communications staff.

- [ ] **Large dominant companies** have an even greater need to humanize their communications.

- [ ] **Engineering-oriented companies** need professional and creative communicators to make complex ideas comprehensible to the public.

- [ ] **No matter the scale of the crisis,** there is a positive path forward if your actions uphold your values.

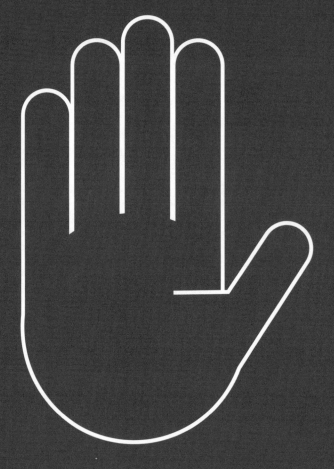

SIEGE
MENTALITY

Craft the narrative you want to project, and demonstrate it through action.

6

ARUBA UNDER SIEGE

"When you have that window of opportunity called a crisis,
move as quickly as you can, get as much done as you can.
There's a momentum for change that's very compelling."
—Anne M. Mulcahy, Former Chair and CEO, Xerox

In 2005 the island of Aruba was inundated with bad publicity after the disappearance of 18-year-old Natalee Holloway, an American teenager visiting on a high school graduation trip. The island nation, part of the Kingdom of the Netherlands, was hammered by international media for its ineffective response to the crisis, for the unresolved questions about Holloway's fate, and for the alleged mismanagement of the resulting criminal investigation. Holloway's body was never found, and the authorities were unable to successfully prosecute the leading suspect, Joran van der Sloot, a Dutch national living on the island at the time.

The stakes in these events were especially high for Aruba, because public safety is integral to its tourism brand. Almost uniquely in the Caribbean, its rocky landscape and dry climate never supported a plantation-oriented economy, and largely for that reason it lacks the sharp class and wealth divisions that have led to high rates of crime and poverty on many other Caribbean islands. This relative harmony and Dutch-flavored stability is so central to the island's identity that its tourism brand, "One Happy Island," is imprinted on all the island's license plates. The Holloway disappearance, which generated enormous media coverage in the United States, thus threatened the island's core brand and identity. Travelers from the United States represent about two-thirds of the island's tourism industry, and the island claims the largest percentage of repeat visitors of any Caribbean destination.

But then, as if that weren't bad enough, the stakes were raised after a second disappearance of an American woman led some in the media to suggest that an ominous pattern was developing. My team and I were brought to the island in 2011, shortly after 33-year-old Robyn Gardner went missing while supposedly snorkeling with her traveling companion, Gary Giordano. Gardner became the second female American tourist whose body could not be found. The story was compelling to American media, some of whom darkly hinted at human trafficking and drug dealing. And Aruban officials, mindful of the criticism they received for allowing van der Sloot to leave the island, imprisoned Giordano and were holding him while they decided whether to charge him in Gardner's disappearance.

The Aruban officials had learned in the 2005 events that it was harmful to have too many people speaking for the island government, too many leaks, and too much gossip feeding the media. But for the Gardner episode, it overreacted and adopted a siege mentality. The government established a policy that only the solicitor general, who functions as chief prosecutor, could speak on the investigation and the related tourism issues. That muzzled tourism officials, private sector representatives of the tourism industry, and their corresponding communications resources. It also had the unfortunate effect of designating a lawyer named Taco Stein, whose brusque manner and clipped Dutch accent was ineffective on American television, as the spokesman for the island.

MANAGING THE MEDIA CIRCUS

When we arrived, a media circus was already under way, and Aruban officials were desperate to handle the situation competently and protect the island's reputation. We immediately encountered the siege mentality that created an information vacuum, not to mention the fact that the solicitor general was not trained in communications or media relations. It created another, more practical problem, for us: our client was not the Aruban government in general, but the Aruba Tourism Authority, which just recently had been converted from a governmental agency to a semi-autonomous organization. While the ATA wanted to respond to the crisis and protect the tourism industry,

A CRISIS WILL THREATEN YOUR CORE BRAND AND IDENTITY.

it had hardly any freedom of action as long as the government was clamping down on its ability to speak. We realized that to achieve the ATA's objectives, we would need to convince the government to recognize the harm that was being created by this vacuum.

Fortunately, the new ATA structure still provided a role for the minister of tourism, who attended our initial meetings shortly after we arrived on the island. We made a presentation to him that emphasized the importance of a more effective and proactive approach that would include not only more freedom of action for the ATA but also media training and message development for Stein as well as for tourism officials. The minister agreed and arranged for us to make a presentation the next day to Aruba's prime minister and his cabinet. This was an opportunity beyond anything we had expected, and we recognized that it could transform the entire government's response to the crisis. We worked overnight to develop a presentation that included a discussion of the principles of crisis communications in the digital age, strategies for protecting Aruba's reputation, and how to improve crisis preparedness. We emerged from those meetings with a mandate for change.

At this point, the clock was ticking on the release of Giordano, who was being held in a prison on the eastern end of the island. Giordano was under suspicion for a variety of reasons, including concerns about the truthfulness of his account of what happened and questions about the nature of his relationship with Gardner. Under Dutch/Aruban law, he could only be held a limited length of time without being charged, and it was becoming clear that the government did not believe it had sufficient evidence to charge him.

Meanwhile, cable news host Nancy Grace had made the Aruba story her cause célèbre and was reporting on the investigation daily. She was highly critical of the Aruban authorities and framed the story in the context of the earlier Holloway disappearance, which she characterized as having been mishandled.

We helped the Tourism Authority get ready for the likely release of Giordano by providing media training for Solicitor General Taco Stein and by planning the Aruban response to the ensuing media onslaught. We also helped craft messaging to make it clear that the Gardner case was not a random crime that posed a threat to the security of visitors. Giordano did indeed leave the island, attracting a media frenzy, but the Aruban authorities did a much better job than in the 2005 crisis. Stein performed well on an NBC News *Dateline* show devoted to the Gardner story, and the hour-long show was as positive for Aruba as we could have hoped.

DEVELOPING NEW SKILLS

Next, we drafted a plan for the Aruba Tourism Authority to modernize its communications through developing skills of key staff members in the organization and to build trust by investing in relationships with the media and other key constituencies. We needed to harness digital strategies and tools to better protect the island's reputation and improve crisis preparedness.

We also conducted digital communications training for key members of the tourism authority staff and then planned a social media and crisis management boot camp for various tourism affiliates, such as tour operators, hotels, restaurants, and transportation companies. The boot camp included an overview of social media platforms, best practices for crisis management, an analysis of the online conversation concerning Aruba, and recommendations for implementing a digital listening and engagement strategy. Using the combined social media networks of multiple Aruban tourism organizations, we enlisted the support of the thousands of loyal Aruba visitors, who return year after year, to post favorable comments and photos.

As a part of our communications strategy, we helped identify and train a new spokesperson for the Aruba Tourism Authority, a woman with a strong command of English who was more comfortable on camera.

Our team at ICF also designed and conducted a full crisis simulation that enacted a refinery explosion and an ensuing power blackout and environmental threat on the island. The simulation included Facebook, Twitter, and other social media posts in addition to simulated coverage on CNN, YouTube, local news outlets, and other media.

Within the exercise we designed an escalation index to help manage responses to natural disasters, crime, disease, environmental threats, and other potential challenges. In each scenario, we built a decision tree to guide the scale of a response and a potential course of action.

To prepare for future emergencies, the ICF team created a 40-page crisis handbook for the Aruba Tourism Authority and the industry, which covered initial actions in a crisis, building a situation room, standby statements for various contingencies, and fast facts on the island and visuals for use in an emergency.

CRISIS EPILOGUE

Gary Giordano was never charged with a crime in Aruba. A year after he left the island, he was charged with indecent exposure in Maryland, although charges were later dropped. AMEX Assurance Company, a subsidiary of American Express, sued Giordano to void a $3.5 million insurance policy that he purchased on the life of Robyn Gardner prior to traveling to Aruba.

Joran van der Sloot, the chief suspect in the Natalee Holloway case, is now serving a 29-year sentence in Peru for the murder of a young Peruvian woman.

Aruba's tourism industry has recovered and reached new milestones over the years. But the Aruban people continue to be deeply affected and saddened by the episode, because these isolated incidents did not reflect the attitudes, values, and culture of the island.

The Aruba Tourism Authority has emerged from the events with a much stronger communications team—equipped with the digital wherewithal—to confront a crisis in the future.

TAKEAWAYS

- [ ] **Once an organization feels as if it has been burned** by the media, it's easy to overreact and adopt a siege mentality. That doesn't work.

- [ ] **The public will often give you the benefit of the doubt** when you experience a crisis—the first time. If such a crisis recurs, the public—and the media—will consider it part of a pattern, and your response needs to be much more robust.

- [ ] **If you have the wrong spokesperson,** you'll feel like you're wearing handcuffs in a fistfight.

- [ ] **Fairly or not, cross-cultural communications** pose special challenges. Attention must be given to such things as English-language skills, the effects of accented English, and even the gender of the speaker.

- [ ] **Imposition of a siege mentality** can deprive employees and stakeholders of the digital tools needed to rapidly respond to a crisis. In the Aruba situation, not only the Aruba Tourism Authority, but also hoteliers and other tourism businesses, needed the ability to use digital channels to reassure customers and respond to inquiries.

☐ **Because TV is such a powerful medium,** there's a tendency to think any mainstream channel is representative of the entire media coverage. But you need to consider the actual size of cable markets before you allow a single network or show to influence your media strategy. In the digital era, you must understand who the real influencers are, and sometimes it's not cable news.

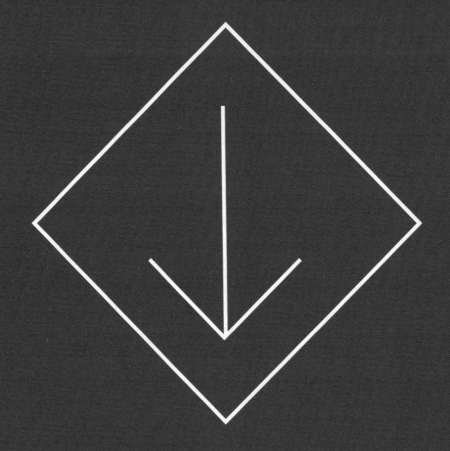

THE URGE TO BUNKER DOWN

Don't do it!

7

—

'FESS UP WHEN YOU MESS UP

*"In any moment of decision, the best thing you can do is
the right thing, the next best thing is the wrong thing,
and the worst thing you can do is nothing."*
—*President Theodore Roosevelt*

In some crises, there is a strong urge to bunker down—to stop
engaging, to resist releasing information, and to shut down the
lines of communication. It's human nature. Sometimes we just get
frustrated, clam up, and stop talking. Most of us have seen it happen in personal interactions. We've also watched major corporations seemingly bury their heads in the sand. But it's never a good
response to crisis.

Many of the biggest public relations disasters contain an element of bunkering down. It has become less common than in the past because in a digital world, there's nowhere to hide. Merely shutting down the outgoing communications doesn't end the conversation. It just leaves you out of it and abdicates the narrative to others. Someone will be happy to fill the information vacuum if you don't.

In some crises, there is a strong urge to bunker down—to stop engaging, to resist releasing information, and to shut down the lines of communication. It's human nature. But it's never a good response to crisis.

While you're losing control of the narrative, you're also losing time: time to shape perceptions; time to create content that will tell your side of the story; time to counter inaccurate reporting and innuendo. By the time you *do* start communicating, counter-productive external narratives may have gotten established, and you're stuck playing catch-up.

So the biggest takeaway regarding the bunker down mode is, don't do it. This seems obvious, but let's explore why otherwise intelligent people might decide to bunker down.

- Sometimes the paralysis results from the fear of not having enough information. For example, in the case of a product

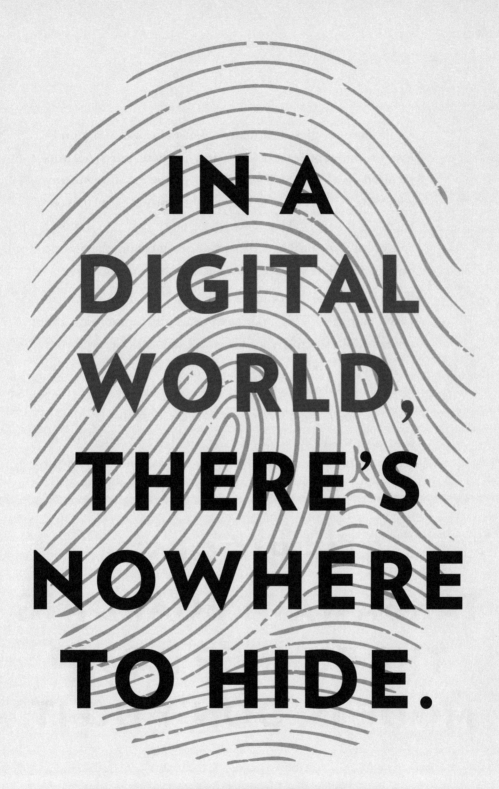

IN A DIGITAL WORLD, THERE'S NOWHERE TO HIDE.

recall there may be uncertainty about the cause of the problem or the proper solution. Also, if there are regulators involved, you may not be free to act without regulatory approvals. This is an example of when process can be your friend. Tell your stakeholders what you're doing to discover and/or solve the problem. Being transparent about the process can buy you time and keep you out of bunker-down mode.

- Then there's the "Let's not stir the pot" or "This, too, shall pass" rationale. This approach takes the optimistic—and unrealistic—view that your crisis will stay unnoticed by your stakeholders. Today we live in an open world where almost everything is discoverable.

- The "us versus them" complex—You can't see the world outside of your bubble and it feels like you'll never catch a break. The resulting beleaguered mindset and sense of victimhood causes you to just turn inward and lick your wounds.

THE BIGGEST TAKEAWAY REGARDING THE BUNKER DOWN MODE IS, DON'T DO IT.

- The failure to accept that you indeed own the problem. One large corporation thought it had isolated a major problem by firing hundreds of employees in its one affected business market. But the mother ship still owned the problem, and it didn't go away.

- The legal liability conundrum—If you admit your mistake you might increase the likelihood or magnitude of legal liability. A triumph of legal advisors over communication strategists may push you into bunker-down mode.

- Stock price—"If we can just wait until the end of the quarter . . ." The fear of adversely affecting an earnings report leads to a delayed communications response.

So it's clear that there are understandable reasons for going silent, but it's almost always a losing strategy. Here are few examples where, on some level, companies shut down communications during a crisis.

BLUE BELL

In February 2015, Blue Bell Creameries became aware that a routine state health department product sampling in South Carolina revealed listeria bacteria in several of its ice cream products. The company quietly began withdrawing suspect product from the distribution system. There was no public announcement. That was soon followed by the discovery of listeria in Blue Bell's manufacturing facilities in Texas.

By March, the Centers for Disease Control determined that a link existed between the ice cream and several deaths from listeria in Kansas. Blue Bell issued a limited product recall. Additional cases of listeria tied to Blue Bell products and further product recalls followed. By April, with listeria cases in Arizona, Oklahoma, Kansas, and Texas, and contamination reported at multiple Blue Bell manufacturing sites, the company recalled all its products and shut down all its facilities.

Critics faulted Blue Bell for "recall creep" and for emphasizing that its products, which were being voluntarily removed from stores, "have not been recalled." There was no apology from the company until April, after all Blue Bell products were indeed recalled. The FDA released inspection reports showing the company had found listeria two years earlier at one of its plants and stated that Blue Bell had not taken adequate steps to eliminate the problem.

Blue Bell would go on to lay off 1,450 of its 3,900 employees and furlough some 1,400 more, according to *Fortune* magazine. Also, the publication reported that "only a $125 million loan commitment from billionaire Sid Bass kept [the company] from going under."

Blue Bell drew criticism for assuring the public, not long after the initial reports, that all its products on store shelves were safe. It was also criticized for not openly addressing the listeria outbreak immediately after the first cases were reported. Texas health department officials fined Blue Bell $850,000 for the listeria contamination.

How might Blue Bell have acted differently? A smaller ice cream company based in Nebraska, Jeni's Splendid Ice Creams, faced a listeria challenge in 2015 and survived it with much less business disruption and damage to the brand. A random sampling of a pint of Jeni's detected listeria, and the company recalled all its products immediately, shut down ice cream production at its plant, and closed all its retail shops until the problem could be resolved. Despite the fact that no illnesses were reported, Jeni's provided thorough information describing the discovery of the bacteria, the measures taken to eliminate the problem, and what consumers should do. It disseminated the information in press releases and on its website, established a specific email account to field consumer inquiries, and extended customer service hours during the recall. The company's updates included detailed information: where the company was in the cleaning process, where the listeria was discovered, how much product was destroyed, and what food scientists at the company were doing to prevent future contamination. Production resumed three weeks later, and the retail shops reopened about a week later.

When listeria was found again later in 2015, production was immediately shut down again. The retail stores were closed for about a week, although it took longer for the sales of packaged ice cream and online sales to resume. No illnesses were reported from either event.

Jeni's benefited from:

- Telling the truth in real time. The public was told what the company knew, when it knew it.

- Supporting the rhetoric with action. Jeni's took immediate, voluntary action to protect consumers, including shutting down all operations until it could ensure product safety. Jeni's lost $2.5 million and 265 tons of ice cream in the first recall, but its actions protected the reputation and long-term welfare of the company.

How could Blue Bell have done better?

- The company wasn't forthcoming about the listeria contamination until after fatalities had occurred. Greater transparency and timeliness would have inspired greater public confidence.

- Blue Bell's recall creep didn't serve it well. It seemed as if the company was telling consumers as little as possible and trying to manage the problem without a costly shutdown and full recall.

- Blue Bell was reported to not have had a chief communications officer or a crisis plan in place. In hindsight, it seems clear that the management team would have benefited from more senior communications staffing and more crisis preparation.

The good news is that Blue Bell enjoyed a strong reputation built on more than 100 years of selling a great product and being a good corporate citizen.

Blue Bell's distribution largely recovered, although it had an additional recall in 2016. Nonetheless customers embraced the return of Blue Bell products, especially in Texas, where the company was founded and where it enjoys a cult-like following.

TARGET STORES

The company's large 2015 data breach of 40 million customers' credit and debit card information was reported by a security news blogger rather than Target itself. Then, in the interest of mitigating liability—or more generously, an incomplete grasp of the facts—the company assured customers that hackers had not stolen their encrypted PIN information. That turned out to be false, and hackers were soon selling customer information on the Internet for as much as $100 per account.

Takeaways: Target should have contacted customers as soon as possible. Why let a blogger frame your message? When it comes to making amends, under-promise and over-deliver. Target got these actions in reverse order when it minimized the breach and had to take back its early customer assurances. It's better to share all the bad news at once rather than disclosing it in installments, which will only prolong the damage to your brand.

NESTLÉ INDIA

Maggi noodles is one of the most trusted and beloved brands in India. In 2014, the instant noodles represented about a quarter of the $1.6 billion annual revenue in India for its parent company, Nestlé. In 2015 a government official tested Maggie noodles for MSG (monosodium glutamate), which the packaging says is not an ingredient. After the noodles tested positive for MSG, Nestlé reasserted its MSG-free claim and requested that the noodles be tested a second

A HIGHER EDUCATION PERSPECTIVE

IT'S ALL ABOUT RELATIONSHIPS

Bill Powers, former President of The University of Texas at Austin

---

Bill Powers, former president of The University of Texas at Austin, had a great deal of crisis management experience in his nine years leading the university. He also had responsibility for one of the strongest brands in higher education. UT is the perennial leader in American collegiate trademark and licensing revenue, and its brand is visible throughout the world.

Building Relationships

"You've got to deal with crisis management before the crisis—by building relationships," says Powers. "Everybody's going to fall down. The question is, will the people around you be there to pick you up or will they kick you?" Powers built strong relationship with lawmakers, alumni, students, and other stakeholders, which were crucial during the "Texas higher ed war" that pitted him against Governor Rick Perry and several members of the UT System Board of Regents.

Break Your Own Bad News

"We experienced a data breach at UT's McCombs School of Business," says Powers. "The dean was in China. We had a meeting on Sunday morning, and someone said we could wait and make an announcement on Monday. I said, 'We're having a press conference this afternoon.' I walked in there and said, 'Somebody broke into the McCombs School computers, and we take responsibility for it. Here's what we're going to do to protect the people whose data has been compromised.' We got very little flak because our alumni learned about the breach from us rather than from someone else."

Sharing a Vision Builds Equity with Stakeholders

"Having a vision and communicating the big rocks to your stakeholders will help you get through a crisis," says Powers. "Your constituents know you believe in the vision, and they're invested in it. Then when there's a crisis, they are more likely to stand with you. You're not consciously shaping a vision in order to manage a crisis, but it helps give you the political capital to weather the storm."

IT'S BETTER TO SHARE ALL THE BAD NEWS AT ONCE RATHER THAN DISCLOSING IT IN INSTALLMENTS, WHICH WILL ONLY PROLONG THE DAMAGE TO YOUR BRAND.

time. Months later the second lab reported not only the presence of MSG, but also seven times the acceptable level for lead. The story was then leaked to local media. Nestlé maintained that Maggi noodles were safe. But rather than communicate directly to customers, Nestlé argued its case quietly through government administrative channels. Many consumers interpreted Nestlé's silence as an admission of guilt.

The scandal spiraled out of control, and in 2015, as Nestlé prepared to announce a national recall, the government banned Maggi noodles as unsafe for human consumption. While continuing to argue that the product was safe, Nestlé destroyed 37,000 tons of Maggi noodles throughout the country. The product was off the shelves for five months.

"This is a case where you can be so right and yet so wrong," asserted Nestlé CEO Paul Bulcke. "We were right on factual arguments and yet so wrong on arguing. It's not a matter of being right. It's a matter of engaging the right way and finding a solution." (Nestlé has always maintained that its noodles were safe.)

Takeaways: Nestlé was very slow to respond to the crisis in social media, losing valuable time to convey key messages. It appeared opaque and arrogant by not responding, and it failed to engage directly with its loyal customer base for far too long. The company also lacked the media relationships and a crisis communications plan to manage the situation. The loss to Nestlé has been estimated at $500 million, and more than a year later sales had still not recovered to pre-crisis levels.

CHIPOTLE

The immensely popular burrito chain was slow to disclose foodborne contamination in 2015 and slow to explain how it would fix the problem. It sparred with the Centers for Disease Control about how the agency released information concerning the outbreak of E. coli in a number of its locations. Chipotle's website and social media channels were silent on the topic in the early days of the crisis. The company ended up closing 49 restaurants in affected areas. Chipotle received blistering criticism for vague notices on the doors of shuttered locations that cited "supply chain" or "equipment" failures. The effects of the incident were more severe for a company which boasted a tagline of "food with integrity." Forty-six patrons were sickened with E. coli, and 20 required hospitalization.

Takeaways: The greater the brand loyalty, the higher the expectations. A year later Chipotle's stock remained down 42 percent from its 2015 high.

THERANOS

This high flyer was once the toast of Silicon Valley. Private investors found the promise of Theranos technology, providing hundreds of medical tests with a single drop of blood, to be irresistible. Led by its young, charismatic, Stanford-dropout CEO Elizabeth Holmes, the private medical technology company stonewalled questions about the workings of its "revolutionary" equipment for months. Holmes, whose net worth was valued at $4 billion in early 2016, was unresponsive to queries about the accuracy and reliability of Theranos' marquee product, a blood-analysis device called Edison.

After incisive reporting by *The Wall Street Journal* and others, it became apparent that Holmes had built a company largely around a concept rather than a reliable product. By mid-2016, the FDA banned the use of Edison, and another federal agency banned Holmes from owning or operating a medical laboratory for two years. *Forbes*, which had described her as one of America's "richest self-made women," later calculated the value of her Theranos stock at zero. Jennifer Lawrence has been cast in the movie version, entitled *Bad Blood*.

Takeaways: Transparency and authenticity help build trust. And once you've lost it, trust is hard to regain. Theranos might have been able to pivot to a different strategy with different products if it had not been perceived as misleading the public, the venture capital community, and the government.

The key takeaway is that going into bunker-down mode is never a good idea. Yet on some level, it still happens every day. Bunker-down mode prevents you from effectively pursuing the five key principles of crisis communications: Transparency, authenticity, speed, agility, and creativity. When you are in the bunker, you've left the playing field and you're destined to lose.

Transparency and authenticity help build trust. And once you've lost it, trust is hard to regain.

BRAND
RECOVERY

8

PENN STATE AFTER SANDUSKY

"It takes twenty years to build a reputation and five minutes to ruin it."
—*Warren Buffet*

Many great organizations will be struck by crisis that is often beyond their control. How you *respond* to crisis, however, *is* within your control. This chapter is about protecting and restoring your brand after the acute phase of a crisis has passed but the reputational damage remains.

One way to look at brand recovery is to consider what is expected of us whenever we make a mistake that harms others. Public expectations are not that different from private interactions when things go awry. We all expect a sincere apology, a genuine effort to make amends, and a resolve to learn from the experience and not repeat the mistake.

In the brand recovery phase, ask yourself these questions:

1. Did you accept responsibility for your role in the crisis?
2. Did you apologize?
3. Did you make amends to the injured parties?
4. Did you articulate the ways your organization intends to avoid repeating the mistakes in the future?
5. Did you use what you learned from the experience to make the world a better place? That is, did your actions contribute to new safety protocols, new technology, improved standards, scientific discovery, or developments from which others can benefit?

In 2012 my team and I were invited to Penn State University to help it recover from what may be the worst reputational crisis among major institutions in American higher education. The

HOW YOU RESPOND TO CRISIS, HOWEVER, IS WITHIN YOUR CONTROL.

WE ALL EXPECT A SINCERE APOLOGY, A GENUINE EFFORT TO MAKE AMENDS, AND A RESOLVE TO LEARN FROM THE EXPERIENCE AND NOT REPEAT THE MISTAKE.

challenge was not only to help restore a great but highly tarnished brand, but also to do so in an exploding digital environment where Penn State's reputation was being hammered on a daily basis. It was necessary to change the destructive tone of the online conversation and to increase engagement with the positive manifestations of the brand.

A COMMUNICATIONS CRISIS FOR THE AGES

The Penn State brand got dragged through the mud for much of 2011 and 2012 and continued to suffer for several years following the Jerry Sandusky scandal. The scandal threatened a lofty reputation that Penn State had earned over more than 150 years. Moreover, it created an unprecedented crisis of credibility across the Penn State system of 24 campuses and its worldwide alumni community of more than 500,000. And the controversy was further complicated by alumni outrage over what some considered as capitulation to the NCAA.

At the time of the scandal, Penn State was in the process of refreshing its brand. The university was striving to reinforce the things that made Penn State distinctive and a source of pride. The exercise became substantially more complex and difficult in an environment that included an interim president, internal audiences with varied perspectives and allegiances, continuous coverage of grand jury actions and criminal investigations in the national media, intense media scrutiny of every move by the institution, and ensuing NCAA penalties. The brand seemed to be under constant attack.

Distilling the Penn State brand to its essence and creating a unifying message in such an environment was a formidable challenge. Clearly, the Penn State community needed something positive to rally around. It was essential that "Penn Staters," as well as potential students, faculty, and peer institutions across country, were reminded of the contributions and achievements the university had made and continues to make in expanding knowledge and serving society, as well as providing opportunity for its graduates.

Target audiences included:

- Current Penn State students, faculty, staff, administrators, and alumni;
- Prospective Penn State students, parents, faculty, staff, and administrators;
- Pennsylvania citizens;
- Pennsylvania legislators;
- Fans and supporters beyond the state.

The branding and messaging challenge included several key objectives.

Increase awareness and engagement around positive messaging for the university—Messaging supporting the positioning would need to be viable for years and could not be perceived as merely responsive to the crisis.

Maintain recruitment and enrollment—Penn State needed to continue its success in recruiting top undergraduate and graduate students as well as faculty from Pennsylvania, the Northeast, and around the world. It was important that PSU continue to attract high-quality recruits in spite of the adverse news coverage.

Maintain pride in the university with key stakeholder groups—The university was in the midst of a $2 billion capital campaign. Its annual student philanthropic effort, the largest in American higher education, was in progress. The branding effort needed to inspire pride at a time when it was in short supply.

Create a collaborative, consolidated marketing and communication structure for coordinating messages throughout Penn State's 24 campuses—Training workshops and evaluations were conducted to inform, train, coordinate, and measure effectiveness of the communications efforts. These workshops included more than 100 marketing and communications professionals across Penn State's two dozen campuses.

ASSESSING THE BRAND

An early task was to analyze the organizational structure, talent and capabilities, collaboration among various units, and the overall expression of the Penn State brand. In 2012 we entered the discovery phase, collecting and evaluating materials, reports, brand materials, marketing research, and the communications efforts of the various units of the university. In addition, we interviewed dozens of stake-holders on the main campus and on the smaller campuses. My team also conducted a peer benchmarking study to examine how other large, public universities organized their central marketing and communications departments and to identify best practices.

To evaluate messaging and branding in print, digital media, and visual communication, we collected materials from more than 50 units from across all campuses.

In our analysis of the expression of the PSU brand, we rated materials based on these criteria:

- Do the materials convey PSU values?
- Do they consistently display the PSU logo?
- Is there a consistent look and feel of the materials (colors, fonts, imagery, etc.)?
- Are they readily identifiable as PSU?

To learn more about Penn State and, ultimately, the story to be told, hundreds of interviews and several large quantitative surveys were conducted with members of the Penn State community—current and prospective students, faculty, staff, administrators, and alumni.

After the research was completed, two problems stood out. First, when asked to give examples of Penn State achievements, the vast majority of respondents had difficulty citing specific traits. "We're just a great university," we heard over and again. Secondly, we learned

BRAND STRATEGY

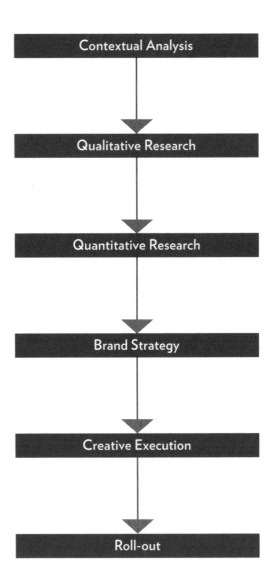

Contextual Analysis

Qualitative Research

Quantitative Research

Brand Strategy

Creative Execution

Roll-out

that many students and faculty outside of the main campus felt disenfranchised. On the 23 other campuses, these important constituents didn't feel as much a part of the Penn State family.

The task became to rekindle the emotional embers intrinsic to the brand and do so in a way that embraced stakeholders on the 23 campuses beyond the flagship.

ASSESSING THE ONLINE CONVERSATION

In order to get a deeper understanding of the brand, we conducted an analysis of the online conversation about Penn State. In November of 2011 there were more than 750,000 online mentions of PSU. Of those, more than 250,000 were about the child sex abuse scandal. Volume began to surge after the arrest of Jerry Sandusky and exploded with the removal of head coach Joe Paterno. Twitter was the most active digital channel. Forty-two percent of the mentions were devoted to the trial and legal proceedings, 15 percent were on the topic of child abuse, 11 percent treated the alleged institutional cover-up, and 6 percent discussed Penn State football. Other topics made up the balance.

RESTRUCTURING THE ORGANIZATION

Our recommendation was to hire a new strategic leader to serve as the chief marketing and communications officer for the university. We helped draft the job description and encouraged Penn State to seek a candidate with private-sector experience who had a strong understanding of digital platforms. A critical function of the position, which would report directly to the president, would be to rebuild, protect, and enhance the PSU brand. We recommended that the University Relations office, which was responsible for central communications, be renamed as Penn State Marketing and Communications.

CRAFTING A BRAND STRATEGY

Penn State needed more cohesive positioning and brand strategy. We helped develop the research to inform the positioning statements and key messaging for the campaign. Cynthia Hall, former Associate Vice President for University Relations and Chief Marketing Officer, stressed that the university was not seeking a new institutional tagline, but instead needed a positioning statement that was both an expression of the brand and that was not closely identified with Penn State athletics.

The campaign needed to connect with the Penn State community, to burnish the Penn State brand, and to encourage Penn State partisans everywhere to defend and take pride in their university. Ultimately, the campaign would reflect a positioning statement that cast the university as a training ground for "Inspired Doers." The positioning statement took this form:

Penn Staters are not only high academic achievers, they're doers—nurtured by a culture that encourages setting lofty goals and investing in the effort to achieve them.

It was necessary for the campaign to capture this spirit as well as inspire unity across all campuses. The campaign tagline that mean "across the university system," "across its myriad programs," or "in the hearts of its students and alumni."

The "Inspired Doers" theme enabled us to build rich content designed for conventional and digital media.

- The campaign provided a means to shine a light on countless PSU contributions that have improved lives in the US and beyond.

- It allowed us to communicate that, no matter where a stakeholder was based, there were Penn State students, faculty, and alumni from all 24 campuses solving real world problems and making a difference.

CAMPAIGN ROLLOUT

The campaign was introduced to internal audiences first. It was launched on Homecoming weekend in October 2013 at the University Park campus and, simultaneously, rolled out on all PSU campuses across Pennsylvania. Creative units developed included:

- Giant "Penn State Lives Here" banners hanging from major buildings on each campus;

- Billboards on highways leading into communities where campuses were located in the major markets of Pittsburgh and Philadelphia;

- T-shirts, flags, lawn and lobby signs, bumper stickers, and electronic display boards;

- Magazine spreads and posters celebrating major research accomplishments;

- A brand video introducing the "Penn State Lives Here" concept (shown at the homecoming game and to alumni during the alumni road show);

- Two 30-second broadcast TV spots;

- A brand style guide for use by campus communications professionals;

- Dedicated storytelling space on the main Penn State website;

- Integrating the new theme in messaging and speeches by key stakeholders, such as at the inauguration of Penn State's new president;

- Establishing a University Branding Council comprised of University executives.

As the new campaign unfolded, we also established ongoing strategic components to ensure that Penn State's messaging and outreach were maintained at a high level.

Upgrade Skill Sets—PSU needed more staff with stronger skills in marketing and communications, including brand development, digital and social media, crisis communications, content creation services, and market research and analytics.

We made recommendations about building a stronger organizational structure and making key hires. Positions were added to provide the targeted skill sets in digital, content creation, and analytics.

Stronger Internal Communications—Improved communication with internal stakeholders was necessary to create greater transparency and to improve the relationships between key internal audiences such as the president's office, intercollegiate athletics, the PSU board of trustees, and key constituents throughout the university system.

In crisis, your own employees are often harmed. They may experience disappointment and embarrassment. Some may lose their jobs, and their pension plans may suffer. Employees can be your strongest brand ambassadors, but only if they understand and can articulate the key messages. I'm reminded of the expression, "Take care of the inside, and the inside will take care of the outside."

Re-envision Digital and Social Media Presence—Penn State developed a stronger team to re-launch its home page and to provide digital strategy and leadership for websites and social media channels controlled by the many units throughout the system.

Develop Performance Management System with Key Metrics—Measuring progress is not possible without establishing key metrics and a baseline. We helped define the key metrics and establish the reporting systems to measure performance. The metrics included brand awareness, undergraduate applications, fundraising, student and alumni engagement, athletics event ticket sales, website traffic, and the sentiment and message penetration within the online conversation.

A BOARD ROOM PERSPECTIVE

WHAT THEY NEED TO KNOW AND WHEN

Bill Cunningham, former Chancellor of The University of Texas System

---

One crucial constituent group in a crisis is the institution's board of directors. William H. Cunningham has observed crisis management from both the perspective of CEO and as a board member. He served as chancellor of The University of Texas System, which includes 14 campuses, 71,000 employees, and an annual budget of more than $10 billion.

Cunningham has served on some 25 corporate boards, including Southwest Airlines, where he is presiding director, insurer Lincoln National, where he is chairman, and John Hancock Mutual Funds.

"Chief executives want boards who are supportive, but they don't want boards who micromanage them," says Cunningham. "The CEO expects to deal with normal problems on a regular basis. What is normal? A big organization like Southwest Airlines or John Hancock often has weekly significant problems. The board doesn't want or expect to get called for the routine problems, because the board delegates that responsibility to management.

"In the case of a major crisis, the CEO would be wise to rapidly contact the board. If for no other reason, this permits the CEO to put his or her spin on the crisis. When I was CEO, I wanted my board to hear about a significant event from me. I wanted to tell them what the problem was and how I was going to solve it."

The Price of Not Communicating

Cunningham says that the roles of the CEO and the board have been well understood at almost all the companies he has served. The one exception did not turn out well for the CEO. "I think it's very unusual for the board to get involved in a crisis. It's one thing to be informed. But as directors, we are not equipped to take the crisis away from the CEO and attempt to manage it. Our responsibility is to see that the CEO does his or her job, and if he doesn't, to replace him. At one of my companies, there was a breakdown in communications between management and the board. When that happens, the CEO has to go. The board always wins."

The digital era has accelerated the pace of communications. "The United Airlines case [involving a passenger dragged from an overbooked plane in 2017] is a classic example," says Cunningham. "The situation was mishandled, but the fact that a video of the incident went viral on social media elevated it from a major problem to a real crisis."

Hiding Doesn't Help

"Crisis communications is very important. Transparency is very important and getting out in front of the story is very important," Cunningham says. "You have to respond to the press, even though at some point, everyone feels that the press is unfair. But that's the role of the press—to hold people in power accountable. People in leadership positions must participate in the communications process. After all, the story *will* be written. Do you want the story to say the CEO was unavailable? Or do you want the article to include your side of the story? The lawyers always preach caution. Sometimes CEOs put more faith in what the lawyers advise than the public relations people. But in a crisis, if you hide, it won't help."

TAKE CARE OF THE INSIDE, AND THE INSIDE WILL TAKE CARE OF THE OUTSIDE.

The outcomes were impressive:

1. Increased Penn State Brand Awareness. A Brand Awareness Survey that sampled the general population in Pennsylvania in early 2014, four months after the launch of the brand campaign, revealed some important results.

   More than 50% of the respondents had encountered a Penn State ad, and 27% had recently seen or heard the campaign tagline, "Penn State Lives Here." The survey also showed that Penn State was rated very highly with respect to key messages regarding PSU's contributions to society and commitment to students and community.

2. Prospective undergraduate applications *increased.* Penn State received more than 84,500 applications for the 2013–2014 school year, an increase of almost 9,800 applications over the previous year.

3. Increased exposure of key messages on the website. The university received more than 310,000 page views of storytelling content during the first few months of the site launch.

4. Increased engagement with alumni. The university completed a $2 billion campaign ahead of schedule as part of the overall institutional response, even while the Sandusky crisis and related news continued to dominate headlines.

5. Increased engagement with current students. Four months later, THON (formerly known as the Interfraternity Council—IFC— Dance Marathon), the largest annual student-run philanthropic effort in the world, raised $13.3 million to fight pediatric cancer, making it the most successful in the school's history.

6. Penn State University Marketing moved from a structure with highly individual silos to a collaborative, comprehensive organization. A Brand Council, a Marketing Council, an alumni road show, and marketing workshops were established.

There is an even more important metric for the overall institutional response that ultimately helped drive restoration. Penn State committed $12 million from the NCAA fine to help establish the Center for Healthy Children, recruiting world class scholars to what has become the preeminent academic center in the country working to solve the complex problem of child maltreatment. The balance of the fine was used to support child abuse programs in Pennsylvania.

These outcomes, which resulted from a devastating crisis, will help fight child abuse in Pennsylvania and beyond. Regardless of the way history judges the various actors and the institutions in the Sandusky case, there will be a positive legacy in support of child advocacy.

Other crises at other organizations have similarly generated enduring positive change.

I praised Johnson & Johnson's response to the 1982 Tylenol case in chapter one for demonstrating authenticity and transparency in a crisis. But Johnson & Johnson was also a pioneer in brand recovery. It established a new standard for product safety by introducing tamper-proof packaging that revolutionized the industry.

Other examples:

- The Tokyo Electric Power Company (TEPCO) has helped lead an international effort that has invested more than

$4 billion in new safety measures to protect the world's nuclear power plants in the aftermath of the Fukushima crisis and is committed to sharing with the world the knowledge and technology being developed for the unprecedented cleanup at Fukushima Daiichi.

Within every crisis lies opportunity. It's our job to recognize opportunities and to help organizations make the most of them.

- New guidelines and improved technology have made off-shore drilling safer following the catastrophic BP Deepwater Horizon explosion and oil spill. BP committed to pay $500 million over 10 years to support independent research to improve society's ability to deal with the potential impacts of oil spills on marine and coastal ecosystems. As of 2015, BP's Gulf of Mexico Research Initiative had awarded approximately $391 million in grants for research in areas including the ecological and human health aspects of spills, and the development of new technology for future spill response and restoration.

Within every crisis lies opportunity. It's our job to recognize opportunities and to help organizations make the most of them.

TAKEAWAYS

- ☐ **In brand recovery,** make sure you:

    - ☐ Accept responsibility for your role in the crisis;

    - ☐ Apologize to the affected stakeholders;

    - ☐ Make amends to the injured parties;

    - ☐ Articulate the ways your organization intends to avoid repeating the mistakes in the future;

    - ☐ Take action to leave the situation better than you found it. For example, TEPCO's actions since the Fukushima crisis have improved safety standards for nuclear power plants all over the world.

- ☐ **Increase communication with stakeholders** during a crisis. This is not the time to be gun shy. Your stakeholders want you to recover, and the public needs to hear what you're doing to make things right.

EPILOGUE

As of this writing, my team and I are working on an active case of cyber extortion. These situations involve hackers installing malicious software that encrypts the target company's data. The infected software threatens the victim's ability to operate—blocking services, transactions, access to records, and other functions. Typically, the hackers demand payment in the form of virtual currency such as Bitcoin, the international cryptocurrency. The ransom transactions are run through an international bank or Bitcoin exchange. The amounts are often relatively small, tempting the victims with expedience versus a long and possibly fruitless investigation. Under normal conditions, most victims would never consider negotiating with criminals.

In our current situation, which involves a healthcare organization, the potentially disruptive effect of the attack has been to temporarily prevent the practices from accessing patient information. Several factors add complexity to communicating about such a crisis.

First, when your data and communications systems have been compromised, it may be necessary to assume that the hackers can see what you are telling stakeholders about the crisis. You may need to scramble to establish an alternative platform for informing and communicating with constituents. In our case, we rapidly launched a microsite to serve as an information hub. And you can't overestimate the frequency with which your stakeholders want updates. We have kept up a cadence of at least two information updates per day. Also, it's easy to be so focused on customers that you overlook employees. Those employees who interact with customers need to be well informed and prepared to discuss the crisis effectively.

Digital extortion and ransomware illustrate how the speed and complexity of crisis management is accelerating and why skilled crisis communication is essential. But no matter how the crisis landscape evolves, you can still expect to experience the six stages:

- Surprise;
- Insufficient Information;
- Intense Scrutiny from the Outside;
- Escalating Flow of Events;
- Siege Mentality;
- The Urge to Bunker Down.

Armed with this knowledge and effective digital tools, you can survive a crisis and successfully defend your brand.

And you will still be well-served by the five principles of crisis:

- Authenticity;
- Transparency;
- Speed;
- Agility;
- Creativity.

Armed with this knowledge and effective digital tools, you can survive a crisis and successfully defend your brand.

ARE YOU READY?

IF YOU ARE A C-SUITE EXECUTIVE OR OTHERWISE RESPONSIBLE FOR AN ORGANIZATION, HERE'S A CHECKLIST TO DETERMINE YOUR COMPANY'S LEVEL OF CRISIS PREPAREDNESS.

1 Do you have a robust listening capability that allows you to monitor and analyze the online conversation about your brand? The online conversation is a proxy for mainstream media. Online listening has replaced the overnight polling that was once used to shape crisis messaging.

☐ Yes ☐ No

2 Do you have an active issue management system—an issue radar—to monitor current threats to your organization?

☐ Yes ☐ No

5 Is your crisis information, including holding statements for the most likely emergencies, in digital form so it can be rapidly deployed across multiple channels?

☐ Yes ☐ No

6 Have you simulated the crises most likely to occur so your team is not wrestling with unfamiliar protocols and systems in the heat of the moment?

☐ Yes ☐ No

CRISIS CHECKLIST

☐ *If you cannot answer all these questions in the affirmative, you are unprepared. Your organization, and your career, could suffer serious consequences when a crisis strikes.*

3 Do you have redundant systems for notifying, gathering, and sharing information with your issue management team when crisis strikes?

☐ Yes ☐ No

4 Do you have rich content describing your people, processes, plants, and places that can be used to fill the information vacuum in a crisis?

☐ Yes ☐ No

7 Do you have a dedicated situation room equipped with everything you need to manage a crisis, sustain the crisis team, and maintain contact with your entire organization?

☐ Yes ☐ No

8 Have you considered building a dark microsite to be activated in times of crisis?

☐ Yes ☐ No

ACKNOWLEDGMENTS

I had the good fortune to start my career at the world's largest and most respected public relations firm, Burson-Marsteller. Founder Harold Burson was my mentor, and I am grateful for the decades of kindness and advice he has generously extended to me.

Burson-Marsteller was home to many pioneers in the business, and I was privileged to work alongside many of them. Al Tortorella, who was deeply involved in the Tylenol product-tampering episode, developed much of the early thinking and insights into effective crisis management. Others included Jim Dowling, former CEO who worked on the Bhopal/Union Carbide disaster, Tylenol, and numerous other crisis situations; Tom Mosser, who lost his life to the Unabomber, Ted Kaczynski; Jim Lindheim, who sent me a much-needed guide to crisis management early in my career when I was wrestling with a crisis in South Korea; and Martin Langford, known as the "Master of Disaster" by the media in the United Kingdom.

And I will always be grateful to my dear friends and past bosses, former CEO Tom Bell and former President Don Cogman.

I also want to thank my many colleagues at PulsePoint Group and ICF. I met Bill Feldman when we were trying to unravel an American company's natural gas problems in Russia. Bill combines a reporter's curiosity and media savvy with an attorney's grasp of the law and an ability to alleviate the concerns of fellow lawyers in the situation room. My old friend and former partner Paul Walker helped introduce me to the digital era as we worked on the largest product recall in the history of the consumer electronics industry. I am also indebted to Bob Feldman, my cofounder at PulsePoint Group. He hired me right out of college and has been a great friend, mentor, and business partner. Grant Toups has been there since the beginning of PulsePoint Group and I'm now proud to call him our Managing Partner. I owe a great deal to Grant for believing in the value of this book for our clients and the industry. James Wakefield is a former student and has been instrumental in developing many of the proprietary crisis management systems that we use at ICF. Zach Irsik, perhaps our longest serving intern, who started in the digital equivalent of our mail room, has provided many insights from the perspective of a Millennial and digital native. There are several other colleagues at PulsePoint Group and ICF who made this book possible, thank you!

Geoff Leavenworth has gone from client, to guest lecturer in my class at The University of Texas at Austin, to confidant and coauthor in the writing of *Brand Under Fire*. And my associate at ICF Karly weekends and vacations over the years—and my children, Christopher and Caroline. The only way I have been able to serve clients in crisis around the globe and around the clock is through the understanding, generosity, and sacrifices of my family.

Jeff Robert Hunt

• SURPRISE

exist in digital form so it can be rapidly deployed across multiple
...nked Word documents do not count as "digital")

...lished and defined the roles of your crisis response team for each of your
...s major areas of vulnerability?

...have a dedicated situation room equipped with everything you need to manage
..., sustain the crisis team, and maintain contact with your entire organization?

...n the last 12 months, have you simulated the crises most likely to occur?

Has your company articulated a cultural point of view on how to respond during a crisis?

STAGE 2 • INSUFFICIENT INFORMATION

Do you have a dark microsite ready for deployment, in case of a crisis?

Do you have holding statements, media Q&A, etc. prepared for each of your
company's most likely crisis scenarios?

Does your company have a predetermined stance on weather it will disclose
information in a crisis?

Does a mechanism exist for keeping company information as up to date as possible (e.g.,
people, protocols, policies)?

Do you have a defined system/channel for notifying, gathering, and sharing information
with your issues management team when crisis strikes?

STAGE 3 • INTENSE SCRUTINY FROM OUTSIDE

Do you have the technology and resources to analyze the online conversation around
the issue as it evolves?

Do you have a digital/social advertising/SEO strategy for when a crisis hits?

Does your organization have defined processes and technologies to prevent version
control around statements, key messaging, etc.?

Has your list of media contacts for global, national, regional, and industry publications
been updated in the last 90 days?

Do you have defined processes to keep employees updated with important information?